Writing News for TV and Radio:
The Interactive CD and Handbook

Mervin Block
and
Joe Durso, Jr.

02   01   00   99   98   5   4   3   2   1

Library of Congress Cataloging-in-Publication Data

Block, Mervin.
    Writing news for TV and radio : the interactive CD and handbook /
Mervin Block and Joe Durso, Jr.
        p.   cm.
    Includes bibliographical references and index.
    ISBN 1-56625-113-3
    1. Broadcast journalism—Authorship.   I. Durso, Joe, 1945–1998.
II. Title.
PN4784.B75W75   1998
808'-06607—dc21   98-41024
                                                              CIP

Bonus Books, Inc.
160 East Illinois Street
Chicago, Illinois 60611

Composition by the dotted i, Bettendorf, IA

Printed in the United States of America

To our students

To Maureen and Joanna
—Joe Durso, Jr.

To Joe Durso, Jr.
—Mervin Block

We are what we repeatedly do.
Excellence, then, is not an act but a habit.

Aristotle

CONTENTS

1

GETTING STARTED

*It's not wise to violate the rules
until you know how to observe them.*
T. S. Eliot

You already know how to write, right? But do you know how to write right? At least, right for broadcast? Probably not. You've been writing letters, essays, reports and other compositions—all intended for the *eye,* for someone else to *read.*

But writing news for broadcast is a course of another color. Broadcast writing is intended for the *ear,* for someone else to *listen to.* But don't fret. No sweat. Not yet. With this book and the interactive CD-ROM, you'll find out *how* to write for the ear, for people who are listening.

So instead of writing a long article, you'll write a mere particle—a compact script. You'll see how to boil down a slew of facts. You'll learn how to make your scripts tight, bright, and read and sound right. And, by the end, you should write right.

As a beginning writer, you already know that writing is work. But you might not realize that you do much of your work before you write—and *after. Before* is when you grasp the ins and outs of writing, *after* is when you spot any flaws and see how you can improve, how you can make your scripts more speakable, understandable, recallable—and commendable.

The best way to do that is to apply the rules. Some of them you know. Some, you may not even know that you don't know. And some, you may not care for. But just as rules govern broadcasting, rules also govern newswriting. So in the interest of better broadcast newswriting, we're going to look at some rules. Not that this is a rule book. Consider it a writer's handbook, a guide to making scripts shorter, sharper, stronger.

1

You may think rules are for use when brains run out. Or that rules can be made only by rulers. So I'm going to rule out any *diktat, ukase,* or *fiat*—none of those European imports. And certainly no *bull.*

Instead, unless my editor overrules me, I'm calling these rules *tips.* My mental computer, though, has programmed them as rules for me. They weren't handed down to me at Mount Sinai; I've never even been in that hospital. For more than 30 years, I've absorbed them while writing in network newsrooms and refined them while teaching in college classrooms.

I shy away from asking anyone else to live by my rules. But I'm not mealymouthed, so I'm not going to say that you *might consider trying* them. I am saying that whatever you call them, you can put them to work for you. And they do work. As many ads for kitchen gadgets say, they're simple, reliable and fully tested. If you apply the rules—no matter how experienced you are—you're bound to write better.

When I started writing news for broadcast, I knew only one or two rules: type on one side of the page, do not split sentences from one page to the next. But over the years, I picked up some sensible rules on newswriting from old pros, I dredged up some from my memory of a college class in broadcast newswriting, and I devised some from insights gained through writing day after day after day. I also assimilated rules laid down by various writing experts, including Strunk and White—and *they* do call them rules.

Besides all the things I learned to do, I learned many things not to do. And I learned a lot from my mistakes. Mistakes are often our best teachers, so the sooner you make your first 5,000 mistakes, the sooner you'll be able to correct them. With all that experience, now I can at least recognize a mistake when I make one.

The tips and reminders—or rules—you'll find in the following pages are omnidirectional: they cover radio and television, and they apply to all kinds of newswriting, from 20-second stories to two-hour specials, from anchors' "readers" to reporters' "wraps."

The work you will do as a broadcast news professional is important, and it's a true challenge, tougher in many ways than writing for print. That's because listeners to broadcast newswriting have only one chance to understand your script; they can't refer to a previous word or sentence; they can't set a story aside and go over it at their leisure; they can't ask you what you mean. But they can turn to another newscast. So as you write, think of your listeners, and write for *them.*

Until now, most of the writing you've done was probably for other people to read. Now it's time to start writing for others to hear.

That may seem to be a simple assignment. But too many newcomers and too many old timers don't grasp the difference between writing for the eye and writing for the ear. That may be because some writers of news for broadcast don't spend enough time listening. That's right, listening—to conversation.

Imagine this: What if you recorded all the conversations you hear for one day, played them back and analyzed the patterns of speech? You'd probably find that when people talk, they (including you) generally don't start sentences with dependent clauses, typically don't use parenthetical phrases, usually speak in the active voice, almost always use simple language and (when the message is important) don't waste words. Unless they're naturally windy. Or else giving a speech, which they probably *wrote* in advance.

People talk to communicate. And because they talk so much, they're accustomed to having information delivered to their brains through their ears in certain patterns, which have become familiar and expected. So when we deliver broadcast news, it's important that our stories flow into our listeners' ears in the same familiar way. That's why we pay particular attention to the grammar, language and sentence structure of broadcast news stories. To be effective—to be easily understood—our scripts must be recognizable to our listeners as *conversation.* So we should write the way we talk. I'm not saying it's desirable to do that, or important, or essential. It's *imperative:* Write the way you talk.

No one writes *exactly* the way he talks or talks the way he writes, so writing for broadcast is a compromise. But keep in mind that you're writing for people who can't read your script, people who can only hear it—and hear it only once. One way to make sure they get it the first time around—and they do get only one crack at it—is to use everyday language.

You don't need to stoop to the style of Dick and Jane, but you should write in a straightforward, linear fashion—without detours or zigzags—so ordinary listeners can grasp it word by word, word for word, word after word. It's that unswerving directness—and adherence to rules—that enables listeners to follow the thread of your story.

You'll learn some of those basic rules for broadcast writing in this chapter. The rules will help you construct good broadcast sentences; the rules were adopted in recognition of how people talk and how they listen:

how they expect to hear words in certain sequences and patterns. So write the way you talk. And follow these rules:

1.1 Go with S-V-O: subject-verb-object.

That's the standard pattern of sentences for people who speak English. The closer the verb follows the subject, the easier for the listener to follow. Start sentences with the subject, go straight to the verb and then the object. The next point follows naturally from this one.

1.2 Don't start a sentence with a participial phrase or any long dependent clause.

If you follow rule number one, this won't be a problem. But it's surprising how often you hear anchors, even network anchors who should know better, read sentences that start with introductory phrases and clauses. But that's not the way we talk. It's not the way anyone talks. And it's not the way to help listeners latch onto a story.

You wouldn't say to a friend,

Needing new shoes, I'm going downtown tomorrow to buy a pair.

No. You'd say,

I need new shoes, so tomorrow I'm going downtown to buy a pair.

Yet, some newscasters do use the type of participial phrase we see in that first sentence.

A lead that backs into a story with a participle is weak and murky. It requires too much of listeners. The participial phrase with secondary information that listeners hear at the start means nothing—not till they hear the next cluster of words and discover what the subject of the sentence is. Then they have to rearrange the word clusters to make sense of what they just heard. How many listeners have the time, energy and aptitude to do that while the wordathon rolls on and on?

Try making sense of this lead, reprinted just as written for a local broadcast:

Saying their project could never be compatible with the river which bears its name, the Regional Planning Council denied approval

of the massive 1800-acre Wekiva Falls Complex in North Orange and Lake County.

If you were listening to that, could you tell what the subject of the sentence is—or is going to be? After such a clumsy approach, would you care?

To make the subject of the story clear and unmistakable, the best pattern for writing your first sentence is subject-verb-object: Start with the subject, go directly to the verb, and follow with the object. The closer the verb follows the subject, the easier for the listener to follow. So go with S-V-O.

1.3 Avoid parenthetical phrases and clauses.

You may think this is repetitious, but I call it reinforcement: the closer the verb follows the subject, the easier for the listener to follow. If you put a parenthetical phrase or clause after the subject, you're separating the subject from the verb. So try to avoid phrases and clauses that separate subject and verb. The greater the distance between subject and verb, the greater the difficulty for listeners. They hear only one word at a time, so that by the time they reach the verb, they have to make an effort to go back mentally and try to figure out who's doing what. While they're trying to do that, they might lose their train of thought. And if they lose it, they probably won't be able to get back on board. And before you know it, they've changed channels and are listening to someone else's newscast.

Consider a listener trying to sort out this imaginary lead:

A million-dollar jackpot winner—*burdened by heavy debts, a critically ill wife and a son accused of beating up a policeman*—shot and killed himself today.

Might sound to some listeners as if a policeman committed suicide. This is an exaggerated example, but it illustrates one of the problems caused by parenthetical phrases and clauses. Do you think listeners—most of whom are only half-listening—can sort that out? And still keep up with the flow of the story?

In re-reading your script, if you find a parenthetical phrase or clause that contains essential information, put it in a separate sentence or incorporate the information in other sentences. Perhaps you could rewrite the lead this way:

A million-dollar jackpot winner cashed in his chips today.

No, I'm kidding. That lead is in poor taste; we mustn't poke fun at someone's misfortune. Try this:

A man who won a million dollars in the lottery shot and killed himself today. He was heavily in debt, his wife critically ill, his son in jail.

When you go with S-V-O, listeners know the subject; they don't have to exert themselves to grasp the thread. And they can hang on to it.

As you write your scripts, always keep this in mind: listeners are not supposed to do the work; you are.

1.4 Put attribution before assertion.

This is one of the hard-and-fast rules that a writer mustn't play fast and loose with. Writers for print routinely place attribution at the end of a sentence, frequently after "according to." Or they tag the tail of a 25-word sentence with "she said."

Broadcast writers, though, must keep in mind that they're not writing for the eye but for a much different receiver, the ear. So in broadcast writing, attribution goes up front, where it would occur naturally in conversation.

When we talk to each other, we automatically put attribution first. We don't stop to think about it. Our conversations follow the S-V-O pattern naturally and spontaneously: "Jim told me, 'Blah, blah.' And Jane replied, 'Hah, hah.'" Is any other word order suitable? Nah, nah.

In the unlikely event your teacher rebukes you, you might complain to a friend,

Professor Smith told me today I have to learn how to park my bike straight.

Without thinking twice, you'd put the attribution first. You sure wouldn't blurt out:

"You have to learn how to park your bike straight." That's what Professor Smith told me today.

Yet, we frequently hear anchors start a story with a quotation—or a an indirect quotation or a stunning statement—and it sounds as if they're expressing their own views:

Good evening. The United States should bomb Moscow back to the Stone Age.

Then the second sentence pulls the rug out from under the opening:

That's the opinion of Councilman Tom Troy.

The opinion of a councilman? Does his area of competence extend beyond his ward? My opinion: that's unfair to listeners. They should know up-front who's doing the saying so they know how much weight to give it. And also so they don't think the anchor himself is sounding off.
And we shouldn't say:

The budget is in good shape, *according to the mayor.*

Correct:

The mayor says **the budget is in good shape.**

Here's another type of hard-hitting lead we often hear with no preceding attribution:

Anyone who chews five sticks of gum a day can ensure healthy gums and teeth. That's the finding of a study done by researchers in Asuncion, Paraguay, and it shows that. . . .

All it shows is that some newspeople should work harder at understanding how people speak. And how they listen.
We don't credit the wire services for their material because, in a sense, they work for *us.* If a wire service moves a big story that seems improbable, a network will quickly try to pin it down itself. If a networker cannot verify it and the story is too big to ignore, a newscaster will start the story this way:

The Associated Press says **the chief justice of the United States is going to undergo a sex change.**

If the story were less startling, or less unlikely, the broadcaster might delay identifying the source but would make clear that the information is not in the realm of established fact:

The chief justice of the United States *reportedly* **plans to retire soon.**

The next sentence would explain *reportedly* by linking it to the people doing the reporting:

The Associated Press also reports he's going to move to Hawaii.
The A-P says the chief justice has told associates he wants to. . . .

That's the same way we handle big stories broken by newspapers:

The chief justice of the United States *reportedly* is entering a monastery. *The New York Times also reports* he plans to. . . .

No responsible news organization wants to say, on its own authority, with no confirmation:

The chief justice of the United States is entering a monastery.

Nor does it suffice—having already jarred the listener—to report the chief's impending departure and then say:

That's what the *New York Times* reports today.

But don't overdo attribution. Not every story, let alone every sentence, needs attribution. When you have a story where the facts are indisputable—say, two cars collided on Main Street—you probably need not attribute the story to police. But if police say one driver had been drinking, or police affix blame, you'd better attribute that assertion to police.

When attribution is essential, it should precede the assertion. Experts, seldom unanimous, agree on this principle, which I've reduced to three words: Attribution precedes assertion.

1.5 Activate your copy.

Start with action verbs. Write in the active voice.

If your copy lies there limply, give it some get-up-and-go with verbs that move. When you write in the active voice, the subject of the sentence acts. The passive voice is weak because the subject of the sentence doesn't act but is acted upon. Use of the passive often conceals the actor:

Mistakes were made.

Or,

A cherry tree was chopped down.

Another fault: besides concealing the actor (also known as the doer or agent), the passive voice is wordy. And dull.

Don't confuse passive *voice* with past *tense*. They're different. You can detect the passive voice by looking for a "to be" helper verb followed by the past participle of a second verb:

Final exams *will be taken* by all journalism students in May.

Another tip-off that you're dealing with the passive voice is when the doer in the sentence follows the verb, as the students do in the sentence above. Or, when the doer (he, she or they) is missing altogether:

Final exams *will be taken* in May.

By freshmen only? By students who haven't earned a "B" average so far? By graduating seniors?

The passive voice is frequently a result of incomplete reporting. A sentence that uses the passive voice often leaves out important information, like "who did it?" So be a thorough reporter. Then make it active:

All journalism students *will take* final exams in May.

In some cases, comparatively few, if the subject is more important than the act or the actor, the passive may be preferable. You wouldn't dash to the microphone, for example, and report (in the active voice):

John Wilkes Booth just *shot* President Lincoln.

The reaction to that bulletin would be "Huh?" In this case, the passive voice is appropriate:

President Lincoln *has been shot.*

In that example, the President is clearly more important than the man who shot him. And there may be occasions when you don't know right away who did a deed. Then you have little choice but to use the passive voice until you find out. But as I've said, use of the passive voice in a script often follows newsgathering that isn't thorough. So before your next newscast, you'd better find out who did it.

In their classic *The Elements of Style,* Strunk and White say, "The active voice is usually more direct and vigorous than the passive." And they offer an example:

Passive: At dawn the crowing of a rooster *could be heard.*
Active: The cock's crow *came* at dawn.

Even better (our example):

The cock crowed at dawn. (Shorter, sharper stronger.)

Strunk and White go on to say, "When a sentence is made stronger, it usually becomes shorter. Thus, brevity is a byproduct of vigor." And that's our goal for sentences: shorter, sharper, stronger.

Strunk and White's point about brevity highlights another bonus that comes with writing in the active voice whenever possible: save a few words here and there throughout a half-hour newscast, and, before you know it, you make time for another story. So when you write your newscast in the active voice, it's easier to understand, and it has more news in it.

I wouldn't say, "The passive is to be avoided." As an activist, I say, "Avoid the passive."

1.6 Use present tense verbs where appropriate.

The verb that most often can be used in the present tense is *say*. You might even be able to use the present tense throughout your story, or you might shift in the second or third sentence to the past tense. Example:

Governor Hawley *says* he's going to visit China. His goal, he *says*, is to push for business for the state's farms and factories. The governor *told* a dinner audience in Middletown tonight that he *plans* to leave the first of next month.

Note: In the second sentence, the attribution is delayed. That's all right because the first sentence led with attribution. It is O. K. to defer attribution until after the first few words; it's definitely a no-no—make that No-No—to defer attribution until the *end* of any sentence.

A newspaper or wire service reporter might end a sentence with "the governor said" or "according to the governor." But people don't talk like that, and we broadcasters don't write like that. The second sentence in that example does need attribution because we don't really know what the governor's true goal is; it may be no more than a free vacation.

1.7 Place the time element, if you need one, after the verb.

But you should ask yourself, "Does this story need a time element? If so, do I need to put it in the lead?"

The listener who turns on your newscast tonight has every reason to believe that all your news is today's, not yesterday's, not tomorrow's. What *will* catch the listener's ear and prompt him to keep listening is an action verb, not a time element like "today."

But sometimes the time element is essential. When it is, put it after the verb, not before it. For example, don't write:

> **The president and Republican congressional leaders *this afternoon* reached agreement on a balanced budget.**

That sounds unnatural. And it is. Now, this sounds conversational:

> **The president and Republican congressional leaders reached agreement *this afternoon* on a balanced budget.**

But even in this case, is a time element really necessary in this lead sentence? It's much stronger to write this lead not in the past tense but in the present perfect tense, like this:

> **The president and Republican congressional leaders *have reached* agreement on a balanced budget. They emerged from the White House *this afternoon* all smiles . . .**

Starting the story that way puts the news up top without any clutter in the lead. What's important is that they've reached an agreement. During which part of the day is secondary. Keep all secondary information out of your leads, including the time element.

Using *yesterday* in a lead is foolish; listeners want to know what went on today and, better yet, what's going on right now. If you're dealing with a yesterday story, write a second-day lead: start with the *today* angle. If it's a *yesterday* story that has just come to light, focus on *today's* disclosure or use the present perfect tense:

> **A man *has been shot* dead. . . .**

If you must use *yesterday* or *last night* to avoid misleading listeners, use it in the second or third sentence. (But in an early morning newscast, use of *last night* in the first sentence of a story is often acceptable because it doesn't date the item noticeably.)

Whatever you do, don't put two time elements in the same sentence. This network example presents the worst of times:

> **The Chinese Air Force pilot who crash-landed his twin-engine bomber in South Korea *last night today* asked for political asylum in Taiwan.**

Better:

> **The Chinese Air Force pilot who landed his bomber in South Korea *has asked* for political asylum in Taiwan.**

Once again, using the present perfect tense has helped us avoid an unnecessary time element.

So always ask yourself, "Do I really need this time element in the lead?" Time after time, the answer will be "no."

1.8 Limit a sentence to one idea.

This makes it easier for listeners to understand a story they can't read, let alone reread. By limiting a sentence to one idea, the writer serves listeners by uncomplicating stories, by simplifying (but not over-simplifying) them, by reducing difficult, complex stories to their crux.

1.9 Use short words and short sentences.

Think small. The words that people use most frequently tend to be short. We don't want to use baby-talk, but we do want to make ourselves understood by people who may be only half-listening, people who may be listening amid distractions, people on the go, people who have a lot on their minds, people who have no opportunity to check your script, people who can't rip out your story and go over it at their leisure—or ask you what you mean. People are accustomed to hearing words the same way they absorb them in an ordinary conversation, in a linear fashion, and they are best able to understand them that way: short words in short sentences. People are more comfortable with short words. That's why some big words have been bobbed: "telephone" *(phone); *"airplane" *(plane),* "parachute" *(chute),* "automobile" *(auto* or *car),* "refrigerator" *(fridge),* "tele-vision" *(TV),* "air-conditioning" *(a.c.* or *air).*

When you write your next script, keep these basic rules of broadcast writing in mind. Soon, you'll see how they help make your copy more lively, more listenable and more memorable.

But if you want to win a Peabody and not wind up a nobody, here's another important rule: Don't be intimidated by rules. Newswriting isn't an exact science. To improve your scripts, go ahead: bend a rule or break one—if you must. But only when you can improve a script.

First, though, you must *know* the rules and *know* when you're break-ing them. As the poet T. S. Eliot said, "It's not wise to violate the rules un-til you know how to observe them."

2

WORDS TO WATCH OUT FOR

Strip language clean,
lay it bare down to the bones.
Ernest Hemingway

The word is out that in many newsrooms the word is in. Words are indeed on news directors' minds: surveys show that almost all of them say the skill they prize most in newcomers is writing. And news directors have told me they're paying closer attention to what's being written. That's good news for good writers; they'll never go hungry—not if they have the write stuff. You have my word.

Good writers pay attention to every word, because newscasts don't contain many of them. Words eat up time, and if time is money, wordy writers are worth less, or worthless. That's why it's so important to write with precision, to make every word count, to avoid wasting the time it takes to say a needless word, or a wrong word, or a word that doesn't carry its weight.

Good writers examine every word in a script and keep in the front of their minds the admonition: **If it's not necessary to leave a word in, it *is* necessary to leave it out.**

Here's some wordwatcher's advice that will make your writing shorter, sharper, stronger.

2.1 Eliminate time-wasting words.

Not only do excess words waste time, but they also dilute the impact of what we say. Some words are usually excess baggage. So watch out for:

14

In order—as in "They went to the White House *in order* to protest the president's action." In most cases, when we delete *in order,* the meaning of the sentence is the same.

In the process of—as in "The mayor is now *in the process of* deciding whether to run for another term." When you delete *in the process of,* the meaning is the same; and the sentence is improved.

Literally, actually, really—as in "The umpire *literally* walked off the field." Or "The sheriff *actually* saw the crash." Those adverbs don't help. So they hurt. *Really.*

Suddenly, gradually, finally—as in "*Suddenly,* he fell off the roof." No one falls gradually. Remember that scene in Hemingway's *The Sun Also Rises* when Bill asks, "How did you go bankrupt?" And Mike replies: "Two ways. Gradually and then suddenly." *Finally,* those adverbs add nothing to a sentence but bulk. *Usually.*

Flatly—as in "She *flatly* denied it." and "He *flatly* refused." A denial is a denial. A refusal is a refusal. So *flatly* falls flat. In *The Careful Writer,* Theodore M. Bernstein calls *flatly* "almost always superfluous."

Personally, officially—"The governor *personally* favors taking steps to stop the project." *Unofficially,* those adverbs only delay delivery of the news. Another adverb that's usually unnecessary is *formally. Seriously.*

Miraculously—Leave miracles to ministers. If you get the urge to write "*Miraculously,* no one was killed," try "Somehow, no one was killed."

Local and nearby—as in "The injured were taken to a *local* hospital." Or to "an *area* hospital." (*Area* is rarely an adjective, except in "area code" and "area rug.") Where else would the injured be taken? To an out-of-town hospital? If someone is taken to a distant hospital, it may be worth reporting. Otherwise, listeners assume the injured were taken to the nearest hospitals. A nearby hospital isn't worth mentioning. But when anyone is taken to a hospital across the street, that may be part of the story. Ambulances *take* people; scripts shouldn't *rush* them. Ambulances do rush; so do firetrucks. That's their job. But in copy, *rush* sounds breathless. And please don't write that the injured were taken to three *different* hospitals. All hospitals are different.

We hear anchors say,

The indictment says the defendants met on seven *separate* occasions.

Separate is superfluous. Of course, the occasions were separate. Otherwise, the defendants would have met only once. Better:

The indictment says the defendants met seven times.

"*Separate* occasions" and "*different* hospitals" are common lapses to which a good writer cannot be indifferent.

A total of—as in "*A total of* 50 people were hurt." A total waste.

Then—as in "After he was arrested and charged, he was *then* freed on bond." When the chronology is obvious, *then* tends to be unneeded: "After he was arrested and charged, he was freed on bond."

The fact that—as in:

The marchers were protesting *the fact that* the sheriff refused to release the two prisoners.

Better:

The marchers were protesting the sheriff's refusal to release the two prisoners.

When you eliminate *the fact that* from a sentence, you almost always improve your script. That's a fact.

2.2 Use familiar words in familiar combinations.

Using familiar words is not enough. We have to use them in ways that listeners are accustomed to hearing. A broadcaster recently said,

The economy shows growth signs.

All good, plain words—but: We don't talk that way. And, I hope, don't write that way. We'd say,

The economy shows signs of growth.

2.3 Don't use non-broadcast words.

A non-broadcast word is one not readily understood by most listeners. A listener who's baffled by a word on a newscast isn't going to reach for a dictionary. How many listeners understand *infrastructure?* Or *draconian?* Or *byzantine?* How many *writers* do?

I remember a network anchor's asking me the meaning of *evanescent.* I knew. But I didn't know whether he knew and was testing me or just was avoiding a trip to the dictionary. Maybe he figured that if I knew, everyone knew. So he went ahead and used *evanescent* in his newscast. What we write is indeed evanescent, *fleeting.* But *evanescent* is a non-broadcast word. So is *vagaries.* How many listeners know what they are? Or confuse them with vagrants?

I don't have a complete list of non-broadcast words, but here are some warning signs: if you suspect that a word you're considering is a non-broadcast word, you're probably right. If you've never run into the word before, never used it and never heard anyone else use it, or if you have to look it up in the dictionary, it's a good word *not* to use. Some newswriters think that by slipping in a big word or an off-beat word they'll make a big impression. On whom? Their boss? Their audience? Well, they do make an impression—and it's unfavorable.

We hear *gubernatorial* on the air during political campaigns, but it's a word that deserves retirement. I doubt that anyone outside newsrooms ever uses it. Not even gubernators. And don't dare use obscure or sesqui-pedalian words. The best policy: save big, fancy words for Scrabble.

2.4 Don't use newspaper words.

Broadcast newswriters should avoid newspaper words. Newspapers use them because they're short enough to be shoehorned into headlines. But people don't use newspaper headline words in conversation: *vie, nab, oust, laud, quiz, grill* (unless you're writing about steaks and chops), *foe, woe, fray* (please don't write that someone "was shot in the fracas"), *hike* (as a synonym for *raise* or *increase*), *ink* (as a synonym for the verb *sign*), *pact* (please don't let anyone *ink* a *pact* or ask for a *hike* in her *pact*), *opt, eye* (as a verb), *blast, rap* and *hit* (when they're intended to mean *criticize*) and *up* as a verb: "The workers want to *up* their pay." Which reminds me of a *Reader's Digest* title: "How We Upped Our Income; How You Can Up Yours." All those short words—and others—can be fitted into one-column heads in papers. But they're not words that we use when we talk; even newspaper copy editors don't *speak* them.

Slay is another newspaper word we should kill on sight. *Slay* is a good Anglo-Saxon word, but *slay* is not so strong as *kill* or *murder.* And *slay* isn't conversational. I don't know anyone who says *slay.* Nor do I know anyone who uses the past tense, *slew,* or the past participle, *slain.* So don't use *slay* unless you're talking about dragons. Or Santa.

Also: when writing about a young person, don't call him, her or it a *youth,* as in "Police are also questioning the youth about several other murders." It's not uncouth to say *youth: youth* has long been used to describe a young person, especially a young man between boyhood and adulthood. But *youth* is a print word, not a broadcast word. Have you ever used it in conversation? Do you ever hear anyone else use it? If so, please report him to the Bureau of Youth Abuse.

Other words commonly used in print that shouldn't be used in broadcast copy but are used: *former, latter, respectively.* Why not use them? Because few listen to and remember names or items mentioned even moments earlier; and they certainly can't look at your script to see what you were referring to.

Another newspaper word that's not a broadcast word: *accord.* Some broadcasters use it because they don't want to repeat *contract* or *agreement.* But have you ever heard anyone outside a newsroom say *accord* (except in a Honda showroom)?

2.5 Delete hollow words.

Hollow words are often combined with words that do matter. But the hollow words just take up time, space and energy. They're nothing but padding. These extraneous words, when used in certain combinations, include *incident, activity, condition* and *situation.* Newscasters talk about "the shooting *incident*" when all they should say is "the shooting." (Incidentally, a shooting is hardly an incident. An incident is usually a minor event, such as a jostling on the bus.) Also, don't write about "the famine *situation.*" A famine is a famine. And everything is a situation. We're in one right now.

Some weathercasters refer to "thunderstorm *activity*" when they should say only "thunderstorms." They may say "the storm *condition*" will last several hours. That sentence, too, would be stronger if it were un*conditional:* just say "the storm." We hear weathercasters talk about the temperature's reaching "the 45-degree *mark.*" By itself, 45 *degrees* is enough. And "the temperature's falling to zero *degrees.*" Zero is on the thermometer, but zero is not a degree. Zero is zero.

Newscasters also talk about a trial that has been "one month *long.*" Better: "The trial has lasted a month." We hear about an attorney who needs *one month's time.* But we have no time for *time.* And no need for it. Some newscasters may say:

The test will run for a three-month *period.*

Better:

The test will run three months.

Period!

2.6 Shun vague words.

One of the most popular is *involved*. When I hear that someone was *involved* in a crime, I don't know whether that person committed it or was a victim. Or a witness. Whenever possible, be specific.

2.7 Avoid vogue words.

Several of these buzzwords and fad words that shouldn't find their way into your copy: *accessorize, arguable, high-profile, icon, interface, meaningful, methodology, paradigm, parameters, parenting, prioritize, pro-active, scenario, supportive, viable.*

2.8 Terminate weasel words.

I'd change the slogan "Never say die" to "Never say *pass away.*" You may think you're being more solemn and respectful by saying someone *passed away*. Or *passed*. Or *passed on*. Or *succumbed*. No. Those euphemisms may be well intended, but they're wordy and indirect. So hereafter, when dealing with the hereafter, just let people *die*. And if you're tempted to use *expired*, perish the thought. Save *expired* for contracts and subscriptions. The nice-nellyism may be well intended, but it's merely wordy and indirect. (Even hairstylists prefer euphemisms: "Never say dye.")

Some squeamish writers also say "attack" instead of "rape," but an attack covers many kinds of assaults. So stop squeaming.

2.9 Keep away from windy words.

Some newswriters use windy words either to inflate their stories or because they're not aware of simple synonyms. They use *commence* when they could say *start*. Maybe they think *start* is too common and that they ought to give their copy a touch of class. But there's no point in putting on airs. Windy words just slow down listeners' comprehension, add length to a story and dilute its impact.

Other highfalutin words that we hear too often: *utilize* instead of *use; implement* (verb) instead of *carry out* or *put into effect; implement* (noun) instead of *tool.* And please don't use *initiate,* unless you're writing about a fraternity. We have no need to say *approximately* when all we need is *about.* Mark Twain said, "I never write 'metropolis' for seven cents when I can get the same . . . for 'city.'"

2.10 Drop weary words.

A weary word has been used up through overuse. The first one that comes to mind, and it comes to many minds, is *controversy.* That's why so many newscasters refer to a *new controversy,* or to a *controversial* candidate, a *controversial* bill, a *controversial* plan, a *controversial* move, a *controversial* movie, a *controversial* action, a *controversial* faction. Almost everything is controversial. Even Santa Claus. Some people object to him because they regard Christmas as a sacred day, not to be mocked by Santa and his commercial ties.

So who or what is *not* controversial? Congress debates bills, people argue over candidates, objectors circulate petitions, and pickets protest. Broadcast newswriters who want a strong word for a lead may reach for *controversy* or *controversial* because they think it's the best and fastest way to go. But they don't realize that the more they use *controversy* and *controversial,* the less those words mean.

2.11 Never use wrong words.

Make sure you know what a word means before you use it. The best way to make sure is to check a dictionary. One of the most frequently misused words in scripts is *dilemma.* It doesn't mean *problem, plight* or *predicament.* A *dilemma* is two alternatives that are equally undesirable.

The ten other most misused words, according to a *Los Angeles Times* survey: *egregious, enormity, fortuitous, hopefully, ironically, penultimate, portentous, presently, quintessential, unique.* Another word that's often misused is *heroics.* Dictionaries define *heroics* as "talk or behavior that is excessively dramatic and intended to seem heroic." So *heroics* shouldn't be confused with *heroism.*

Other words we should steer clear of include *pled,* misused as the past tense of *plead.* The preferred form is *pleaded* (consult your *Associ-*

ated Press Stylebook and Libel Manual). And use the preferred past tense of *sink (sank), shrink (shrank), fit (fitted), broadcast (broadcast), dive (dived)* and dozens of other verbs. Watch out for regular *and* irregular verbs—and other irregularities.

And keep an eye out for words with contrary meanings, like *sanctions.* When newscasters say the United Nations' "imposed sanctions," they mean "penalties." But in most dictionaries, the first definition of the noun *sanction* is permission or approval. The fourth or fifth definition, depending on your dictionary, is "a penalty." The verb *sanction* means "allow." So the use of *sanctions* in a script can leave listeners in a quandary.

Another word to watch out for is *depose,* which means "to remove from office or power." But *depose* also means "to take a deposition from." So if you write that an official was deposed, your sentence may be ambiguous; and an editor who sanctions ambiguity should be deposed.

Also watch out for sound-alikes, words that sound the same but have contrary meanings, like *raze.* To raze a building is to tear it down. But a listener hears *raise* and thinks a building is going up, not coming down. And "to *halve* pollution" is far different from "to *have* pollution."

2.12 Forget foreign words and phrases.

Many listeners have all they can do to understand basic English. Surveys estimate the number of illiterates in this country at more than 20 million. And not everyone classified as literate is a prospective Ph.D. So writers should stick to English, the only language we expect listeners to know. Most listeners don't read the *New Yorker* and don't work the *New York Times*'s crossword puzzles. And, except for immigrants, most of us don't use or hear foreign words in conversation. The people we're writing for are people who understand only one language, English. Plain English. So let's stick to everyday words. Every day.

I don't want to seem persnickety, but we should also avoid *per.* No, that's not a peremptory command. As with other tips, rules, principles, or whatever you call them, I'm not saying, "never, ever, under any circumstances whatsoever." All I'm saying is, whenever possible, avoid *per.*

Most experts oppose the use of *per* where *a* or other familiar English words will do. For example, instead of writing "55 miles per hour," write "55 miles an hour." Instead of *per week, per pound,* write *a week, a pound.* And avoid *per se, per annum, per capita, per diem* and *per deum*—unless you write with divine inspiration. Also avoid *amicus curiae, caveat emptor, en route, gratis, ipso facto, quid pro quo, status quo, via, vis-à-vis,* etc., especially *et cetera.* Avoid almost all other Latin words and terms. I say *almost* all because a few are so deeply rooted in our common speech that they are acceptable, such as *percent.* It comes from the Latin *per centum,* meaning "by the hundred." But use *percent* only *after* a number. Not "A large *percent* of cooks were out of work." But "A large *percentage* of cooks were out of work."

A few Latin words may be acceptable *in extremis* when no English equivalent is available or when the Latin can be readily understood. The Latin term *in absentia* may be acceptable to report the case of a defendant who was sentenced when not present. At least, *absentia* sounds like *absence.* But I think it would be better to say "He was sentenced although [he was] not present." Or "although he didn't show up." Another acceptable Latin term is *persona non grata,* the diplomatic term for someone declared unwelcome—not to be confused with *persona au gratin,* a diplomatic big cheese. Otherwise, foreign words are just not *à propos.*

The columnist Mike Royko once took a swipe at Americans who use foreign words: "Just as irritating as restaurants are books and magazines that slip French words in and expect us to understand them. That's why I gave up reading the *New Yorker,* which is one of the worst offenders. I don't know why that magazine does it. Half of all New Yorkers I've known can't speak understandable English, much less the language of the bwah and fwah."

Not only should newswriters avoid foreign words, but we should also avoid words with roots in Latin or Greek. Instead, whenever possible, we should use words of Anglo-Saxon origin. So let's not use the verbs *exonerate* (clear), *extinguish* (put out), *facilitate* (help, ease), *endeavor* or *attempt* (try) and *triumph* (win). And let's not use the nouns *insurgent* (rebel), *conflagration* (fire), *altercation* (fight), *lacerations, abrasions* and *contusions* (cuts, scrapes and bruises). Exception: though it's a blend of Greek (from the word for "at a distance") *and* Latin (from the word for "see"), our listeners should have no trouble understanding the word *television.*

Another language to steer clear of is the language of lawyers, exemplified by *therefore* and *nevertheless.* No need for a newswriter to use any of them. Here are the basic English equivalents: *therefore* = so; *nevertheless* = even so; *notwithstanding* = despite. Also, skip *however.* Instead, use *though, yet, still* or, most often, *but.*

2.13 Pass up clichés.

One cliché is not worth ten thousand pictures. The usual picture a cliché brings to mind is that of a lazy or weary writer. So much copy is clotted with clichés it curdles the mind. A Los Angeles TV newswoman reported that an executive was confident that the movie industry, stung by an investigation, would get a "clean bill of health." I'd like to see one of those bills of health, clean or soiled. Or one of those "bargaining tables" I hear about so much. Or a "bargaining chip." Or even a bargain.

A New York City TV reporter, covering a double murder, said, "The police have their work cut out for them." Made me wonder whether the victims had been dismembered. Another reporter said three fugitives had everyone on "pins and needles." (That script should have been spiked.)

Often, when a blackout, blizzard, flood or shutdown hits a community, a newscaster says residents are "taking it in stride." I've never heard that anyone is *not* taking it in stride.

A network newsman keeps calling gold "the yellow metal" and silver "the gray metal." But I haven't heard him call copper "the red metal" or U.S. currency "the green paper." Yet.

Another cliché: *met behind close doors.* As in: "The president and his national security adviser *met behind closed doors.*" Where else would they meet? On a bench in Lafayette Park? Some writers even have people *huddling behind closed doors.* If the secrecy of a meeting is unusual or significant and worth mentioning, you can say, "The committee met in closed session." Or "met in secret." Or "met privately." But don't let people *huddle* unless there are eleven of them and one is a quarterback.

Also objectionable in news scripts are catchphrases lifted from commercials: "As for your umbrella, don't leave home without it." My advice: Don't reach out and touch any of them. And avoid—almost all the time— song titles and lyrics. How many times have you heard this lead-in to a voice-over, "It rained on the city's parade. . . ."? How many times have you written that? Promise not to do it again?

The most cliché-clotted copy I've ever heard on the air: "[A candidate] *dropped the other shoe* today and *threw his hat into the ring* for president, and now it's *a whole new ball game.*" As Shakespeare put it, and he *was* tuned in: "They have been at a great feast of languages, and stolen the scraps."

When it comes to scrapping clichés, experts disagree. Several experts say some clichés have *a saving grace.* In *The Careful Writer,* Theodore M.

Bernstein of the *New York Times* said: "Use a cliché only with discrimination and sophistication and . . . shun it when it is a substitute for precise thinking."

But many other writing experts say clichés cause air pollution. For them, all clichés are *dead as a doornail.* The columnist Colman McCarthy told how, as a college English major, his required reading list was crushing. So he adopted a method suggested by the writer John Ciardi: "Read a writer's essay, poem, story or column until the first cliché. At that collision, stop. Then drop."

The grampa of good grammar, Henry W. Fowler, also condemned clichés. But he said writers would be needlessly handicapped if they were *never* allowed to use, among others, *white elephant, feathering his nest, had his tongue in his cheek.* In *Modern English Usage,* he observed, "What is new is not necessarily better than what is old; the original felicity that has made a phrase a cliché may not be beyond recapture." (As George Burns put it, "If you stay around long enough, you become new.")

Occasionally, a figure of speech, like a metaphor or simile, can make copy come alive if it's fresh or at least not stale. Too often, though, writers fall back on a device so worn out that its fizz has fizzled.

Although no central registry keeps track of every use of a metaphor (an implied comparison) or simile (explicit comparison), even half-listeners might sense that "war of words" is one of newscasters' most overworked metaphors. A word doctor would pronounce it a dead metaphor. If it's only overworked, it needs a rest; if it's dead, it needs burial. Yet a network anchor recently reported that someone had "triggered a war of words."

The first use of "war of words" is attributed to Alexander Pope (not to be confused with Pope Alexander). According to *The Oxford English Dictionary,* the English poet used "war of words" in 1725. That makes the metaphor more than 270 years old. Even Milton Berle wouldn't take material that old—not even from a Youngman. As for "trigger," it's so overused, I avoid it unless I'm writing about Roy Rogers' horse.

"Metaphor" comes from the Greek word for transference, and Pope has been praised for his ability to transfer the fury of fighting to talking. For the first recorded use of this comparison, he certainly deserves credit. And so does the first wordwatcher who recognized Pope's imaginative phrase and used it himself (with or without credit). But over two-and-a-half centuries, it has become a warhorse, trotted out so often by so many writers that it has become worn out.

Instead of striving for originality and disdaining clichés, unthinking writers turn every clothesline quarrel, as we used to call a backyard shouting match, into a "war of words."

These overkillers should be reminded of Strunk and White's advice in *The Elements of Style:* "Use figures of speech sparingly." Orwell put it more sternly: "Never use a metaphor, simile or other figure of speech which you are used to seeing in print."

Some that fit Orwell's injunction are listed by Harold Evans in *Newsman's English.* Here is a partial list of what he calls "stale expressions":

bewildering variety	lashed out
bitter end	leaps and bounds
brutal reminder	left up in the air
built-in safeguard	lending a helping hand
burning issue	matter of life and death
checkered career	move into high gear
cherished belief	not to be outdone
city fathers	over and above
conspicuous by its absence	pros and cons
cool as a cucumber	proud heritage
coveted trophy	red faces
crack troops	red-letter day
daring daylight robbery	reduced to matchwood
deafening crash	64,000-dollar question
doctors fought	spearheading the campaign
dramatic new move	speculation was rife
finishing touches	spirited debate
fly in the ointment	spotlight the need
foregone conclusion	storm of protest
given the green light to	upset the apple cart
hook or by crook	voiced approval
in full swing	wealth of information
in the nick of time	

If we use those phrases in casual conversation, no one is going to get his *nose out of joint.* But if we use those phrases in news scripts, we risk being written off as hacks. "They [clichés] are so smooth from wear," says *The Written Word,* "that they slip off the tongue or pen with great ease, and that can be the undoing of an unwary writer or speaker. . . . The temptation [to use them] is great merely because many of the expressions in question are catchy (or once were), and to an untrained user of language their surface appeal and never-ending appearance may seem a recommendation in itself . . . *Do one's thing, bite the bullet* and *keep a low profile* suggest that such expressions seem to age very fast through relentless use." That guide's list of clichés includes:

agonizing reappraisal	separate the men from the boys
agree to disagree	separate the sheep from the goats
as a matter of fact	sick and tired
by the same token	silver lining in the cloud
brave the elements	stagger the imagination
bright and early	sweet smell of success
calm before the storm	take a dim view of
can't see the forest for the trees	that's for sure
easier said than done	truth is stranger than fiction
fall on deaf ears	uncharted seas
few and far between	understatement of the ____
go over the top	view with alarm
handwriting on the wall	what with one thing or another
hit the nail on the head	when all is said and done
hit the spot	[more is said than done]
hue and cry	when you come down to it
if the truth be told	wide-open spaces
in no uncertain terms	you can say that again
it stands to reason	you win some, you lose some
land-office business	you're damned if you do, you're damned if you don't
on cloud nine	your guess is as good as ____
part and parcel	
point with pride	
rain cats and dogs	

The journalism educator Curtis D. MacDougall offered some figures of speech (in *Interpretative Reporting*) that he said "are whiskered with age and mark their innocent user as callow":

ax to grind	crying need
blessing in disguise	hail of bullets
clutches of the law	in the limelight

police combing the city
slow as molasses in January
threw a monkey wrench into

watery grave
worked like Trojans

His book also lists what it calls "shopworn personifications:"

Dan Cupid
Father Time
G.I. Joe
Jack Frost
John Q. Public

Lady Luck
Man in the Street
Mr. Average Citizen
Mother Nature

Some metaphors and clichés can be classed as journalese, the super-ficial style of writing characteristic of many newspapers and magazines. Professor MacDougall's list of words that have lost their effectiveness through repetition includes:

brutally murdered
death car
feeling ran high
gruesome find
infuriated mob

mystery surrounds
police dragnets
sleuths
swoop down

Other words and phrases in that category are presented by E. L. Cal-lihan in *Grammar for Journalists:*

a shot rang out
caught red-handed
fusillade of bullets
grilled [unless you're writing
    about a barbecue]
hail of bullets

miraculous escape
pitched battle
pool of blood
reign of terror
shrouded in mystery

Still more trite expressions are listed by Richard D. Mallery in *Grammar, Rhetoric and Composition:*

as luck would have it
beat a hasty retreat
clear as crystal

deadly earnest
doomed to disappointment
dull thud

Grim Reaper
irony of fate
it stands to reason
looking for all the world like
method in his madness

powers that be
psychological moment
riot of color
venture a suggestion

The editorial consultant Albert Toner has listed hundreds of once-bright words and phrases that have lost their luster and become clichés. "How many of these tranquilizers," he asks, "do you mistake for stimulants?"

back-to-back
back to basics or square one
    (or the drawing board)
beautiful people
can of worms
close encounters of any kind
collision course
comparing apples and oranges
conventional wisdom
couldn't agree more/care less
cutting edge
cutting-room floor
different drummer
doing something right
down the tubes
extra mile
eyeball to eyeball
fast lane
fat city
father figure
forget it
game of inches
game plan
garbage in, garbage out
goes with the territory
hard ball
hearts and minds
hit the ground running

interestingly enough
like gangbusters
mind-boggling
moment of truth
name of the game
nation that can go to the moon
only game in town
one-on-one
Operation Whatever
pecking order
Project Anything
psychic income
reinventing the wheel
rubber chicken circuit
says it all
since sliced bread
single most
slippery slope
smart money
smoking gun
state of the art
tell it like it is
tip of the iceberg
up for grabs
very private person
wall-to-wall
where it's at
won't fly/wash

The *Associated Press Guide to News Writing* lists more:

beauty and the beast	long arm of coincidence (law)
beyond the shadow of a doubt	paint a grim picture
bite the dust	pay the supreme penalty
blazing inferno	picture of health
blessed event	pre-dawn darkness
blissful ignorance	proud parents
bull in a china shop	radiant bride
club-wielding police	rushed to the scene
colorful scene	scintilla of evidence
dread disease	spotlessly clean
drop in the bucket	sprawling base
glaring omission	supreme sacrifice
glutton for punishment	tender mercies
last but not least	trail of death and destruction
leave no stone unturned	walking encyclopedia
limp into port	

How many of the following trite expressions have you heard in newscasts? They're among many listed in *Words into Type,* a reference book for editors, published by Prentice Hall.

aired their grievances	long-felt need
beginning of the end	masterpiece of understatement
built-in safeguards	proud possessor
charged with emotion	ripe old age
failed to dampen spirits	shot in the arm
grind to a halt	superhuman effort
herculean efforts	unprecedented situation
hurriedly retraced his steps	untiring efforts
ill-fated	vanish into thin air
iron out the difficulty	voice the sentiments
keep options open	wrapped in mystery
leaves much to be desired	young hopeful
lend a helping hand	

As far as exhausted expressions go, that's not *the whole kit and caboodle, not by a long shot.* But those samples provide enough *food for thought* to help writers think more about what they write—which is, after all, *the bottom line.* One of the most fertile fields for clichés is the athletic field. Sports writers, says Callihan, must learn to avoid words and expressions like these:

battled furiously	pellet
chalked up a victory	pigskin
charity toss	pill
horsehide	rifled the ball
in the shadow of their own goal posts	tangle with

Some sports writers seem to think that writing in simple English might cause them to be benched, so they do their double-barreled damnedest. They say a batter has *belted a four-bagger, clouted one for the circuit, poked one out of the park,* or hit a *roundtripper, a tater, a goner, a dinger,* even a *grand salami.* (I never sausage a thing.) They'll go to any lengths— even *the length of two football fields*—to sidestep simplicity.

The sports producer William Weinbaum tells of a few old standbys that sportscasters rely on to avoid that dreaded word *homer:* "You can hang a star on that baby," "It's see-ya-later time" and "That dog will hunt." Intent on grandstanding, they ignore the easiest—and best—way to say it: "He hit a home run." After some of the offenders condescend to write "hit," I recommend they learn to use "win"—as a verb. I keep hearing about teams that *triumphed, grabbed a win, rolled up a victory,* or *handed a defeat to.* I'd like to hear more about teams that just *won.* And teams that simply scored runs, goals, baskets or touchdowns. "When sportscasters try to be too cute," Weinbaum says, "they come across as clowns." And imitators come across as clones.

Even more tiresome is the use of sports jargon in non-sports news. So resist the lingo of the jargonauts, where all the world's a game and all the men and women merely players.

Some political writers are more guilty than sports writers. Here are some of the political clichés that ricochet and re-echo through our minds, clichés that we should not use at the drop of a hat in the ring:

Front-runner. Put it on the back-burner. Who knows for sure which candidate—or non-candidate—is ahead until all the delegates or voters have cast ballots? As an article in the *Washington Journalism Review* said, "Hart's New Hampshire surprise did not show that reporters need better ways to pinpoint the leader; it showed the error of trying to do so at all." (When Senator Gary Hart dropped out of the race for the presidency in 1988, it was called a *Hart-breaker.*)

Hart attack, Hart-stopper, Hart failure. Bypass 'em. Puns on people's names age rapidly. And most people whose names lend themselves to puns have heard them all—many times. Just don't "Kick that Block!"

The last hurrah. When Edwin O'Connor wrote *The Last Hurrah* in 1956, the phrase was fresh. But it has long since gone stale. Like *It's all over but the shouting,* it deserves its own bye-bye.

An idea whose time has come. When Victor Hugo (or his translator) wrote, "Greater than the tread of mighty armies is an idea whose time has come," he expressed an idea with originality. But his line has been trampled by his followers' footsteps. Even the variations since it was written in 1852 have become tiresome: "an idea whose time has come again," "an idea whose time has come and gone," "an idea whose time will never come." For all of them, original and variations, time has run out.

The right stuff. Clichés don't have it.

On the campaign trail. Too tired for *the comeback trail.* Why not merely say the candidate is campaigning?

On the hustings. It's an outdated and wordy way of saying someone is on the road campaigning. What *are* hustings? And where are hustings? (Not to be confused with the Battle of Hustings or Hustings-on-Hudson.)

On the stump. Worn to the stump.

A real horse race. Fits the definition of a cliché by Eric Partridge: "So hackneyed as to be knock-kneed and spavined." When tempted to use it, just say neigh.

Political warhorse. Ready for pasture.

Neck and neck. Ditto.

Won his spurs. Pack it away with the buggy whip.

Homestretch. Save it for Hialeah.

Beauty contest. Save it for Atlantic City.

Dark horse. Has been ridden into the ground, but because it packs a lot of meaning in two short words, still good for more outings. (Didja hear the one about the dark horse that won a beauty contest? A chestnut came in second. That, of course, is a color of another horse.)

Political animal. A bone-weary critter ready for the glue factory.

Stormy petrel. Out of petrol.

Crossed the Rubicon. Next time it crosses your mind, ask the first five passersby what the phrase means.

Stemwinder. That word may still be a favorite of politicians and political reporters. But I've never heard anyone else say it—or understand it. Its time has passed.

_____ *is expected to win.* Expected by whom? As Confucius should have said, "Man who lives by crystal ball ends up eating glass."

Warts and all. See a dermatologist. Better yet, a dictionary or a thesaurus. What's wrong with calling an appraisal "frank" or "blunt?"

Has worn two hats, kept a high profile and *kept the political pot boiling.* They're all burned out.

Political litmus test. How many listeners know what a litmus test is? It flunks *the acid test.*

Current incumbent. A redundancy. An incumbent *is* the current occupant of an office.

Margin. It's not a cliché, but it is a word that reporters covering polls and elections misuse often. If Clyde gets 500,000 votes and Merrill gets 400,000, some reporters would say, "Clyde won by a five-to-four *margin.*" Wrong. He won by a five-to-four *ratio.* A margin is the difference between two sums (100,000); a ratio is a proportion.

Open secret. If it's open, it's no longer secret.

Topic A. Passé.

Flushed with success. Use it only if you're writing about a prosperous plumber.

Bandwagon is a cliché I wouldn't retire (even if needs new tires). It works: it's not wordy; it saves many words. It presents a clear, colorful picture. And it's a lot shorter and faster than this definition of *bandwagon* (from William Safire's *Political Dictionary*): "a movement appealing to the herd instinct of politicians and voters to be on the winning side in any contest."

What constitutes a cliché is the subject of a verse printed by Roy Copperud in his *American Usage and Style:*

> If you scorn what is trite
> I warn you, go slow
> For one man's cliché
> Is another's *bon mot.*

I don't want to inveigh against all clichés, but I do want to veigh in against almost all of them. When they were coined, they might well have sparkled. Their popularity, though, has been their undoing; now they're tarnished. They may be tried and true (like that cliché) but they're so trite they lack bite.

2.14 Don't stretch for synonyms for words that are easily understood.

Many writers dread using the same word twice in a 20-second story, not to mention twice in one sentence. Perhaps they fear that someone in charge might think that using *said* twice in a story indicates an anemic vocabulary. So they figure the best way to dispel any such notion is to find a different word for *said.* But in writing broadcast news, the best verb to express oral communication usually is *said* (or *says*).

Says—along with *said*—is part of natural speech. You tell a friend, "Jim says he's going to lunch early." You don't say, "Jim stated [or commented, or observed, or announced, or related, or remarked, or any of dozens of other verbs of utterance] that he's going to lunch early." The word *says* has been compared to a skillful stagehand: he does his work well, moves the show along and stays out of sight.

Some synonyms for *says* cause copy to be either stilted or tilted. Copy that sidesteps *says* is stilted when it uses *states* or *declares.* Those two verbs are best reserved for formal statements or declarations. And copy may be tilted when, as a synonym for *says,* the writer uses a verb that might reflect on the person who was doing the saying, or calls into question his veracity: *admits* ("He admits having a car"); *claims* ("He claims he wrote the book himself") *insists, maintains, complains, concedes.*

Several other verbs are often used as the equivalent of *say,* but they don't have the same meaning. One is *explain,* as in: "He explained that the Bulls won." That's hardly an explanation. *Explain* should be reserved for explanations. *Explain* is not to be used as Ring Lardner did in *You Know Me, Al:* "'Shut up,' he explained."

Point out is another verb not to be substituted for *say.* Save *point out* for pointing to facts, not assertions that may or may not be true. It's wrong to write: "He pointed out that his contract is still valid." He says it is. But maybe it isn't. A correct use for *point out:* "He pointed out that the largest state is Alaska."

Laugh is also used incorrectly as a synonym for *say.* "She *laughed* that losing isn't everything." People do laugh, but they don't laugh words. Better: "She said with a laugh that she would try again" or "She laughed and said she'd try again." And don't let anyone *chirp* even if you're quoting a jailbird who has turned canary.

Some writers who shy away from short words or avoid using a simple word more than once in a script look for what's called an elegant variation. If they were writing about bananas, they would, on second reference, talk about "elongated yellow fruit." It's easier for a listener if we use "banana" twice in 20 seconds. Or even three times. Just don't slip on an appealing variation.

2.15 Leave hot-rodding to the race track.

Hot-rodding is high-powered writing. Hot-rodders pepper their copy with words like *special, major, important, extra, crisis, unique, unprecedented, exclusive.* In certain stories, those words may be apt. But everything can't be special. "Where everybody is somebody," William S. Gilbert wrote, "nobody is anybody."

Hot-rodders ratchet up a spat between two public officials into a *clash.* And they *lash out* at each other. When the two officials meet, it's at a *summit.* Or it becomes a *confrontation* or *showdown.* When an official announces a drive or a campaign against almost anything, it becomes a *war.* So we have a *war* against crime, a *war* against drugs, a *war* against illiteracy, a *war* against pornography, a *war* against scofflaws. After being bombarded by all these *wars,* listeners lose their understanding of war. So far I haven't heard of a *war* against potholes. Or crabgrass. But at this very moment a newscaster in West Overshoe may be preparing to launch one of those wars.

When hot-rodders write about experts, the experts are described *as respected.* Awards are *prestigious.* Fads or trends become *revolutions,* disclosures *shockers,* increased costs *astronomical* (because they've *skyrocketed.*) Two other popular words in the lexicon of hot-rodders: *mystery* and *mysterious.* When I was a newspaper cub (an *ink*ling), I learned that re-writemen used those words when they were short on facts and long on fancy.

No discussion of hot-rodding can ignore *spectacular.* Broadcasters often apply it to fires or to fire footage (and they're not all fire buffs—or firebugs). Hot-rodding sportscasters apply *spectacular* to a baseball player's catch, a football player's run, a tennis player's serve, or a golfer's drive, not to mention the Amalfi drive. In fact, *spectacular* seems to be an all-purpose adjective, one that some writers use whenever they can't think of anything else to hold their audience.

Here's an example of hot-rodding that made the lead confusing and inaccurate:

Five years ago today, with unprecedented fury, Mount St. Helens erupted, decimating 150 square miles of lush green forest.

That's the lead of a story broadcast by a TV network reporter. Although she didn't sign a consent card for this autopsy, she should be gratified that she's contributing to the advancement of newswriting. We can't tell from her lead whether she meant that the fury was unprecedented for Mount St. Helens or for all volcanoes everywhere. In either case, she was wrong.

The most destructive eruption in modern times was that of Krakatau in 1883. The volcano, in Indonesia, generated tidal waves that killed 36,000 people. The *Encyclopedia Britannica* says, "The enormous discharge threw into the air nearly five cubic miles of rock fragments, and the fine dust [caused] spectacular red sunsets all over the world through the following year."

But the *biggest* blowup in modern times was that of Tambora, also in Indonesia. According to the U.S. Geological Survey, Tambora's eruption in 1815 disgorged more than seven cubic miles of material. Mount St. Helens spewed less than one cubic mile. And, more important, the USGS says the 1980 eruption wasn't even Mount St. Helens' biggest blowup.

That reporter would have been on safe ground if she had just told her story without straining, if she hadn't tried to punch it up with *unprecedented.* When an editor sees *unprecedented,* his mental alarm should go off. Other absolutes and superlatives should also set off his alarm: *only, unique, first, fastest, fattest, foulest* and other *est* words. An editor should ask: How do we know this is the world's *biggest* snow cone? Even if we're satisfied it is, does that make it worth reporting? If we can't confirm it on our own, are we attributing it properly? How do we know this is the world's *thickest* waffle? Or that it's the *first* time anyone has hijacked a bandwagon? Is there a central registry that keeps track of everything everywhere forever—accurately? (An exception: sports, where statistics are part of the game, and statisticians seem to record even the cap size of batboys.)

A reporter on the scene of the Mount St. Helens eruption couldn't know or easily obtain the history of volcanoes (unless she's a closet volcanologist). Even the people I spoke with at the Geological Survey had to dig out the information and call me back. But a prudent reporter doesn't trot out *unique, unparalleled, unprecedented, unsurpassed,* or any other such word without knowing that it's correct—*and* worth mentioning.

One way to avoid hot-rodding is not to write on a hypewriter. We want our copy to be calm, clean, clear and crisp, true and trustworthy. And free from sin.

2.16 Ditch double-talk.

Do you ever hear a newscaster speak of an *acute* crisis? Or hear him say *new* record, *controversial* issue, *specific* details or *final* outcome?

If so, you've heard a redundancy, something said superfluously. Using too many words to express an idea or repeating needlessly is objectionable—unless you're talking about Duran Duran, Sirhan Sirhan, Pago Pago or Walla Walla.

Mike Berriochoa of central Washington offers a few redundancies that he has come across: a forest fire that's *fully* surrounded, a burning home that's *completely* engulfed, then *totally* destroyed.

Some other redundancies—in italics—that we should guard against:

all-time record	join/confer/gather *together*
new recruit	*state of* Ohio
new bride	capital *city*
build a *new* jail	*sworn* affidavit
circle *around*	funeral *service*
square-*shaped*	*self*-confessed
green-*colored*	asphyxiated *to death*
large-*size*	smothered *to death*
friendly *in nature*	strangled *to death*
short *in stature*	*originally* established
few *in number*	*first* began
wide variety	*first* built
head honcho	

Some redundancies show up in ads, repeatedly: *advance* reservations, *pre-reserved* seating, *free* gift, *full* quart, *hot* water heater, *new* innovation, *extra* bonus, and kills bugs *dead*.

When we're chatting, we often lapse into careless speech, which is harmless *enough*. "A man who never said an unnecessary word," Bergen

Evans observed, "would say very little during a long life and would not be pleasant company."

Anyone who was in my company might have heard me order a tuna *fish* sandwich. No more. Since a friend pointed out my offense, I've tried to economize by cutting back just to tuna—and hold the *fish*. An anchor who says *tuna fish* shouldn't be canned. But we must guard against wasting words. Air time is precious.

And that's the point of this chapter. In newscasts, economy in language is not merely desirable, it's essential. Redundancies waste time, blur meaning and lessen impact: the fewer words you use to tell a broadcast news story, the clearer and more forceful the communication. Flab weakens communication and crowds out other news. With leaner stories, you can fit more stories into a newscast and make your newscast newsier. And give your listeners more news.

3

THE LEAD WRITER'S
DEADLY DON'TS

The work of writing can be easy
only for those who have not learned to write.
James Gould Cozzens

Too often, the weakest point in a broadcast news story is the starting point—the opening sentence, the lead. Too many limp. Or just lie there. What a waste! The lead is the most important sentence broadcast writers compose. If the lead's a flop, listeners puzzle over it and miss what comes next. Or they change channels. Enough of that and *you*'ll be changing channels—or careers.

Every lead can't be a grabber, but what listeners hear first can be crucial as to whether they keep listening. The first task of the lead writer is determining the essential information that must go into the first sentence of the story. This may seem obvious. But too many leads fail to get to the core of the story right away, or dance around it with a veil of words. As a result, they're neither informative nor tempting. They don't tell the listener what the story's going to be about. And they offer little incentive for anyone to pay attention.

So, your first task as a lead writer is to select the information that's at the heart of the story. Then you need to contruct a lead sentence that's crisp and clear.

If you listen to broadcast news tonight, radio or television, network or local, you'll hear leads that don't work, or don't work as well as they might. Chances are, the writer made one of the common mistakes listed below, the lead writer's deadly don'ts.

3.1 Starting a story with *There is, There are* or *It is.*

Don't. They're dead phrases—wordy and wasteful. The power of a sentence lies largely in a muscular verb. A sentence gets its get-up-and-go from an action verb like "smash" or "shoot" or "kill"—or hundreds of other verbs that express action.

Although *is* and *are* are in the active voice, they aren't *action* verbs. And they don't convey action. They—and other forms of *to be*—are *linking* verbs. They link the subject of a sentence with a complement—another noun or adjective, a word that identifies or describes the subject. Other linking verbs include *have, seem, feel* and *become.* Not one of them has the power to drive a sentence. They only keep it idling. So when you start a sentence with *there is,* you're just marking time until you introduce the verb that counts.

A network evening newscast:

There is a major power failure in the West affecting perhaps as many as seventeen states.

Now let's make that lead read right:

A power failure has blacked out a large part of the West.

Another *there is* lead, this on local television, needs corrective surgery:

There's a train rolling through town tonight. But this is one you definitely won't mind missing.

By deleting *there's,* we make the sentence shorter. And by making it shorter, we make it stronger. The story is about a train, not about *there.* After we lop off *there's,* let's write it right:

A train is rolling through town tonight. . . .

Here's another lead from a network story:

There's growing speculation in the credit markets that the Federal Reserve is going to ease up again in the face of slow economic growth.

First, lop off *There's.* Then rewrite:

Speculation is growing in the credit markets that. . . .

By deleting *There's,* you're making the sentence tighter. And, once again, by making it tighter, you're making it stronger.

Newswriters should strive to use action verbs. This network script illustrates how *not* to do it:

There was another clash in Britain tonight between police and gangs of youths. The latest incident was in the northern London district of Tottenham, where hundreds of youths overturned cars, threw gasoline bombs and set fires. Several policemen were reported injured. The incident followed the unexplained death of a West Indian woman during a police search of her home.

Now let's see where that lead went wrong. The writer had plenty of action that he could have reported with vigorous verbs. Instead, he began with the flabby *There was.* And he weakened the sentence with *another.* Used so soon, *another* makes almost any story less newsy. After all, the main point of the story isn't that the two groups clashed *again.* The story is that they clashed. If it weren't a sizeable clash, it probably wouldn't be worth reporting at all. And the writer sapped a good verb, "clash," by using it as a noun. Further, *youths* is not a conversational word. Another point: the name of the London district is not worth mentioning, nor that it's in the north.

Now let's look at one way to pep up the first sentence of that story:

Hundreds of young people in London went on a rampage tonight: they overturned cars, threw gasoline bombs and set fires.

Which approach sounds stronger?

Many writers use *there is* because it's a quick, easy way to start a story, as in these examples:

There's a big fire near City Hall.

There's a shooting at the courthouse.

There has been a train collision near Dullsville.

Now let's toss out the wordy, murky *there is* and go straight to the news with a vigorous verb:

A fire has broken out near City Hall.

A lawyer has been shot in the courthouse.

Two trains have collided near Dullsville.

These revised sentences are much stronger than the originals because they do away with *there is,* which is indefinite, indirect and indolent. The new leads start with what should be the subject of the sentence. Instead of relying on the static "is," they move the action along with energetic verbs. As David Lambuth says, "If you have a nail to hit, hit it on the head."

A simple explanation for the weakness of *there is* is offered by Lambuth in *The Golden Book on Writing:* "The habit of beginning statements with the impersonal and usually vague *there is* or *there are* shoves the really significant verb into subordinate place instead of letting it stand vigorously on its own feet. In place of saying *A brick house stands on the corner,* you find yourself lazily falling into *There is a brick house which stands on the corner.*" Lambuth goes on to say that in that last sentence, your attention is first drawn to *there is,* and from that to *stands,* which should have the whole emphasis, because it's the one definite statement in the sentence. (Lambuth's book, now in paperback, was first published in 1923. That may explain why *house* is followed by *which* instead of the now-preferred *that.*)

"Both [*there is* and *there are*] are dead phrases and should be used as a last resort," says John R. Trimble in *Writing with Style.* "Eliminating them through recasting," he suggests, "usually results in sentences that are more vivid, concrete and terse. There are many exceptions, though, and this sentence is one of them."

"*There* itself is not bad," says Theodore A. Rees Cheney, "it's the company it keeps that gets it in trouble. *There* usually hangs out innocently on the corner with other idlers, verbs like *is, was, are, have been, had been,* and other weak verbs of being." In *Getting the Words Right: How to Revise, Edit & Rewrite,* he says, "These colorless verbs merely indicate that something exists, nothing about how it exists, how it behaves . . . nothing to pique our interest."

Equally wasteful in starting a script—or sentence—is *It is.* So experts advise against it. (To be precise, against *It is;* usually, it's also a good idea not to start with an indefinite pronoun like *it.*)

When *there* is used with *is* or any form of *to be* to introduce a sentence, *there* is called an expletive. So is *it* when coupled with a form of *to be,* as in *it is.* The wordiness—and unworthiness—of this kind of beginning can be seen in the Latin origin of *expletive:* "added merely to fill up." So the best rule for newswriters is: Make sure your scripts have their expletives deleted.

3.2 Writing a first sentence in which the main verb is any form of *to be,* like *is, was, were* and *will be.*

Don't. It's not wrong, just weak. Sometimes it's acceptable, even desirable, but in most cases, it's best to search for an action verb.

Is, was, were and *will be* are all linking verbs, so they merely link a subject with a complement that identifies or modifies it. Other linking verbs include *appear, become, feel, has, look.* In certain contexts, they may link, but they don't *do* anything. A transitive verb transmits an action to a direct object:

A truck *hit* a school bus.

There, the subject acts on the object. An intransitive verb expresses an action or a state without reference to an object or complement (a noun or an adjective):

A truck *blew up* outside City Hall today.

Is, though, transmits no action.

Here's a sentence I hear on the air occasionally:

The president *is* back in the White House.

Factually and grammatically, the sentence passes muster, but it doesn't cut the mustard. The *is* lacks movement. It merely expresses a static condition, not action. The next sentence is better because it has an action verb indicating someone has *done* something:

The president *has returned* to the White House.

Or:

The president *has arrived* back at the White House.

Yet the use of *is* in a first sentence is all right when the sentence is short and the story big:

Senator Hooper is dead.

Or:

The war is over.

Those sentences get their punch from their brevity and the impact of the news. That first example also benefits from its strong last word, *dead.* *Dead* gains extra impact from being a one-syllable word ending in one of the consonants that can close a sentence with a thud. Or thwack.

Do not confuse this advice against using *is* when it serves as an auxiliary (or helping) verb in the formation of tenses:

Mayor Holmes *is searching* for a new police chief.

Stronger, though, than a verb form that ends with an "ing" is a finite verb, one with a tense:

Mayor Holmes *has started* to search for a new police chief.

But *is* alone merely says someone or something exists or else describes it:

Mayor Holmes is a man with a plan.

Is lacks energy. It doesn't move; it doesn't tell us something happened; it just is. *Is* does have a place in language, but not in a lead.

Shakespeare knew. The great strength of English, the educator Ernest Fenollosa wrote, "lies in its splendid array of transitive verbs. . . . Their power lies in their recognition of nature as a vast storehouse of forces. . . . I had to discover for myself why Shakespeare's English was so immeasurably superior to all others. I found that it was his persistent, natural, and magnificent use of hundreds of transitive verbs. Rarely will you find an 'is' in his sentences. . . ."

And as the poet Robert Graves said, "The remarkable thing about Shakespeare is that he really is very good—in spite of all the people who say he is very good."

3.3 Burying a strong verb in a noun.

Don't. Instead of writing a lead about a "bomb *explosion,*" write: "A bomb *exploded.*" Nouns are the bones that give a sentence body. But verbs are the muscles that make it go. If your first sentence lacks a vigorous verb, your script will lack go-power.

3.4 Starting a story with *as expected*.

Don't. When I hear an anchor say *as expected* at the top, it's usually a story I had *not* expected. Hadn't even *sus*pected. Most listeners tune in to hear the *un*expected. *As expected?* By whom? Not by your average listener. When listeners hear a story begin with *as expected* and the story turns out to be something they did *not* expect, they probably feel they don't know what's going on. Often, when newswriters start with *as expected,* they do so because *they* have been expecting a development. Or their producer has told them to keep an eye peeled for the story a news agency says will be moving shortly. So they've been scanning the wires. And after hours of expectation, the story finally arrives. Without thinking, without considering their listeners—listeners who aren't newshawks, listeners whose reading is limited to the program listings—the writers rush to type the words that have been on *their* mind. And, as expected, they start with that deflating *as expected,* which takes the edge off any story.

Even more of a turn-off than *as expected* is a negative version that I've heard with my own ears—no one else's. It went something like this:

Not unexpectedly, Senator Blather said today he's going to run for reelection.

Another variation:

The *long-awaited* appointment of Judge Michael Mutton to the State Supreme Court was made today by Governor Grosvenor.

It certainly wasn't *long-awaited* by listeners. Probably only by Mutton. (And his Li'l Lamb Chop.)

3.5 Starting a story by saying someone *is making news, is in the news* or *is dominating the news*.

Don't. Without ado or adornment, go ahead and tell the news. That's what a newscast is for. That's why they call it a newscast. Everyone who's mentioned in a newscast is "making" news. So when writers say someone "is making news" or "making headlines," they're wasting time, time better spent reporting news.

Another waste of time is the lead that says someone "made history today." Or "entered history books today." Only historians will decide what was historic. And it won't be today.

Equally pointless is this lead:

They're rewriting the record books today in. . . .

That script is what needs rewriting. Just tell the news. And if someone has broken a record worth reporting, say so—simply.

3.6 Starting a story by saying, *A new development tonight. . . .*

Don't. Every item in a newscast is supposed to be fairly new, based on something newly developed. Some writers try to go beyond that wasteful opening with:

A *major* new development tonight. . . .

What's to be gained by telling people, "I've got news for you"? Friends may say that on the phone, but professionals don't proclaim it on the air.

And don't start a newscast by saying, "We begin with. . . ." As soon as you open your mouth, listeners know you've begun. Equally useless: "Our top story tonight is. . . ." If it's the first story, it should be the top story. Top stories run at the top. So skip that needless opener and go straight to the news. Similarly, don't write, "Topping our news tonight. . . ." Sounds like Reddi-wip.

3.7 Starting a story with the name of an unknown or unfamiliar person.

Don't. Names make news, but only if they're recognized. An unknown name is a distraction. It can't be the reason you're telling the story; you're telling it because that person figures in something unusual. If the name means nothing to listeners, they're not likely to pay close attention and thus will miss the point of your story. The best way to introduce an unknown is with a title, or a label or a description:

A New York City milkman, Gordon Goldstein, was awarded five million dollars in damages today for. . . .

Many stories don't need a name. Without a name, a story flows better and runs shorter. What does an unknown name in a distant city mean to you? Or your listeners? But, if you're writing about a runaway or a fugitive, the name may be essential.

So what's in a name? It depends. Before using a name, ask yourself whether the story would be incomplete without it. Would a listener be likely to phone your newsroom and inquire, "What's the name of that Alaskan you just said was arrested in Hawaii for cavorting in a Chicken Man costume?" (And if the listener says "cavort," try to get *his* name.) It is standard, though, to start a story with the names of people who have titles, prominent people who are in the news constantly: President Whoever, Secretary of State Whatever, British Prime Minister Hardly-Ever. And omit their first names. The same style applies to mention of your mayor, police chief, coroner, governor and maybe a few other public officials.

We can also start a story with the name of someone who has star quality, a person whose name is widely known—in almost every nook and cranny, by almost every crook and nanny. But we use that person's first name *and* precede the name with a label: "The actress Emma Thompson," "the painter Pablo Picasso," "the author John Updike."

We don't use anyone's middle name—unless. Unless we're writing about someone who has long been identified with a middle name, like John Paul Jones. Or Martin Luther King, Andrew Lloyd Webber or Mary Tyler Moore.

Skip initials, too—unless the person you're writing about has long been identified with an initial: J. Edgar Hoover, Michael J. Fox, Edward R. Murrow. Another exception: an initial may be desirable if you are trying to avoid a mixup with a widely known person who has the same (or a similar) name.

Broadcast newswriters customarily omit "junior" and "the second" after someone's name—unless *not* using them could cause confusion with prominent sound-alikes. But there's no need to include someone's first name *and* a nickname. Go with one *or* the other. But *not* both together. It's not conversational. We don't have time, especially for those silly uses of first names with standard diminutives, like Thomas "Tom" O'Connor. Besides, have you ever heard of a Thomas called Sam?

When you do use names, try to use as few as possible so listeners can keep their eye (or ear) on the ball. Overuse of names—sometimes *any* use—leads to clutter. Don't diffuse the focus of a story; keep the listener's mind out of the clutter.

Also: don't start a story with the name of an unfamiliar organization. And watch out for organizations with ambiguous or misleading names.

For example: the imaginary Good Government Group. Listeners can't see those capital letters. They may think those words are your description of a group of dedicated citizens working for good government. Across the country, newsrooms are bombarded with letters and news releases on imposing letterheads—some from phantom organizations. The Good Government Group may be only one man who bought stationery and rented a post office box—to undermine good government.

3.8 Starting a story with a personal pronoun.

Don't. This script started with a personal pronoun, *he,* and kept *he-he*-ing:

> **He walked out of a New York prison today looking a little slimmer and slightly grayer. But one thing has not changed. He's still followed everywhere he goes.**

Who *he?* I want to know from the get-go who or what a story is about. So when I hear a script start with *he,* I wonder whether I missed the first sentence, the one that identified the subject. (That script was broadcast in northern Ohio, so you could say listeners were clueless in Cleveland.) Withholding the identity of the subject stumps listeners. I don't like newscasters to play games with me. And I won't waste time with newscasts that don't present news in a clear, understandable manner. And I'm not alone.

A newspaper feature can start with *he* because a reader can spot who *he* is from a headline or a photo; but we don't open a conversation with a clueless pronoun. If we rely on the best pattern of all, subject-verb-object, we'll avoid premature pronouns.

3.9 Writing a first sentence that uses *yesterday.*

Don't. Listeners tune in expecting to hear the latest news, the later the better. They want to hear news that has broken since they last heard or read the news. Imagine tuning in to an evening newscast and hearing an anchor start talking about something that happened *yesterday.* Yesterday? I thought yesterday was gone for good. Who cares about yesterday? I want to hear what happened today. *Yesterday* is still common in newspaper leads, but for broadcasting, it's too old, too dated, too rearview-mirrorish.

If you must lead with a story that broke yesterday, update it so you can use a *today.* Or use a present tense verb with no *yesterday* or *today.* Or if you find out, just before tonight's broadcast, that the mayor's wife was kidnapped last night, you can write around *last night* or *yesterday* by making use of the present perfect. The present perfect tense expresses an action carried out before the present and completed at the present, or an action begun in the past and continuing in the present:

Mayor Hudson's wife *has been* kidnapped.

In a later sentence, you can slip in that dirty word *yesterday.*

But a script mustn't deceive listeners by substituting *today* for *yesterday,* and it mustn't try to pass off yesterday's news as today's. Use ingenuity in figuring out how to write a first sentence without harking back to yesterday. You don't need to be a historian to know that nowadays, yesterday is history.

A worse sin than using *yesterday* in a lead is using yesterday's news. Try, whenever you can, to give your story a forward thrust, not a backward glance.

3.10 Writing a first sentence that uses the verb *continues.*

Steer clear of *continues* in an opening sentence. In a second or subsequent sentence, *continues* isn't objectionable. But it's meaningless to end a story with "the controversy continues." Or "the investigation continues."

The problem with *continues* is that it doesn't tell a listener anything new. Worse, it tells listeners that nothing's new. *Continues* doesn't drive a sentence or story. It merely says something that has been going on is still going on. It tells the listener this is going to be a story that's not news—just olds.

News is what's new. When you have to write about a long-running story—a siege, a drought, a hunger strike—search for a new peg. If you can't find a new peg, find a different angle of attack, move in from a different direction. Focus on whatever has occurred today or is going on today, something you can report for the first time, something that you didn't know about yesterday. Find a verb with verve, says Merv.

3.11 Starting a story with *another, more* or *once again.*

Don't. With few exceptions, those words are turnoffs. If we start a story with *another,* it sounds as if whatever the story turns out to be, it's bound to be similar to a story told previously, one that's not much different. Perhaps just more of the same.

A broadcast example:

Another jetliner tragedy in Britain today. A chartered airliner caught fire on take-off in Birmingham, and 54 passengers were killed.

The crash is newsworthy on its own merits, not because it was the third airline accident within a month. To punch up that fact, I'd give it a sentence of its own:

A British jetliner caught fire on take-off in Birmingham, England, today, and 54 passengers were killed. It's the third airline disaster in less than a month.

New York City averages about two homicides a day, yet who would think of starting a story, "Another man was shot dead in Manhattan today"? Or "Another tourist was mugged in Central Park today"?

Also, starting a story with *more* signals the listener that what's coming may be more of the same—what some pros call "the same old same old." Usually, it's better to skip *more* and go straight to whatever the new *more* is. One reason many broadcast writers start with *more* is that it's an easy way to go: "More headaches for the president today," "More wrangling in city hall today," "More arrests in the Acme Power case." Want more?

3.12 Starting a story with a sentence that has a *no* or *not.*

At least, try not to. Rewrite your negative lead to make it positive. Instead of saying,

The president is not going to take his planned trip to Tahiti,

you'll have a stronger opening by saying,

The president has canceled his trip to Tahiti.

A basic rule of writing or speaking is: put your sentences in a positive form. In *The Elements of Style,* Strunk and White say that, generally, it's better to express even a negative phrase in a positive way: "did not remember = forgot;" "did not pay any attention to = ignored." Strunk and White urge: "Put statements in positive form. Make definite assertions. Avoid tame, colorless, hesitating, noncommittal language . . . Consciously or unconsciously, the reader is dissatisfied with being told what is not; he wishes to be told what is." (Not for nothing do Strunk and White stress that point.)

Another argument for avoiding *not:* in some cases, a listener may confuse *not* with *now.* We shouldn't go overboard worrying about listeners' hearing problems, but it's the reason some broadcast newspeople write "*one* million" instead of "*a* million"—lest a listener mistake *a* for *eight.*

A similar concern leads many newsrooms to report that a defendant was found *innocent* rather than *not guilty;* they fear that some listeners might not catch the *not.* Or that the newscaster might inadvertently drop the *not.* But many writers (and I'm one) prefer writing *not guilty*—because it's clear and correct. Juries don't find people *innocent.* How could a jury find someone *innocent,* which means without sin?

How about this for a broadcast lead?

A post-convention boomlet is not unexpected and certainly not unwelcome for the vacationing Mondale. . . .

That construction, expressing an affirmative by negating its opposite, is hard for a listener to sort out. And two double negatives in a row, as in that sentence, leave me out of sorts.

Another problem with negative constructions is they often lead to underkill. For example, the first sentence in a story on a network newscast:

There were no surprises at Wimbledon today.

Sounds like an imaginary newspaper banner: "No One Hurt in No Plane Crash." The tennis lead has several faults: it starts with "There were," and says nothing. Although the tennis results may come as no surprise to the newscaster, the average listener would regard them as news. Better:

The tennis star Martina Navratilova was favored to win at Wimbledon today—and she did. She won her fifth singles title there, her third straight.

Prize for negating the positive:

The chairman of the P-L-O, Yasir Arafat, had no kind words for President Reagan today.

No kind words is negative. Be positive. The lead would be far stronger this way:

The chairman of the P-L-O, Yasir Arafat, denounced President Reagan today as "a robot and a parrot."

That old song says it best: "Accentuate the positive, eliminate the negative, latch on to the affirmative, don't mess with Mister In-Between."

3.13 Starting with a quotation.

Don't. Some writers do for a simple reason: going with a quotation is an easy way to start. But it's wrong. And you can quote me.

Quotation leads are wrong on several counts: a listener assumes the words are the anchor's own, people don't talk that way, a quotation is rarely the most important part of a story. And anyway you can probably boil it down and say it better.

It's especially confusing for listeners when the anchor opens with a startling or potentially controversial assertion, like this one:

City Hall needs to be taught a lesson. That's the opinion of a retired councilman, Boris Bravo. He told the council meeting today. . . .

A listener might take that first sentence as the start of an editorial. Better:

A critic of City Hall says it ought to be taught a lesson. The critic, Boris Bravo, is a retired councilman. He told a city council meeting. . . .

3.14 Starting with a question.

Don't. Why not? Opening questions tend to sound like quiz shows or commercials. Questions can be hard to deliver, draw an answer you don't want, and trivialize the news. Also, questions delay delivery of the news. And listeners are looking for answers, not questions. I wouldn't go so far as to recommend that you ban question leads, but I think you should

limit yourself to one every other year. Our job is to answer questions—
not to ask them. So these network scripts start off on the wrong foot.

> **The Achille Lauro is docked safely in Port Said this morning, but
> where are the hijackers? Have they already gone free?**

You're asking us? We tuned in to find out.

> **First, amazement. Then, outrage. Tonight, above all, confusion.
> Who, if anyone, has custody of the four Achille Lauro hijack
> murderers who took partly paralyzed 69-year-old Leon Kling-
> hoffer from his wheelchair, shot him, killed him and tossed him
> overboard? Who, if anyone, will bring the murderers to justice?**

Why the time-consuming hard sell—*amazement, outrage* and *confusion?*
And who's going to stop asking us questions and start telling us what's new?

> **What do Coca-Cola, Caterpillar and General Electric have in
> common? They're just a few of the American companies repre-
> sented in Moscow at a round of talks on increasing U-S–Soviet
> trade.**

How do writers hatch so many question leads that are inane? Questions that no listener could answer, guess at, or even care about? If the
story is worth telling, why not go ahead and tell it?

> **Did Ponce De Leon ever find the fountain of youth he was seeking
> in Florida? A Philadelphia man says he ran into the 500-year-old
> Spanish conquistador back in 1973, and he looked marvelous—
> not a day over 23.**

You don't think I could make that up, do you?

> **What went wrong? That question tonight confronted doctors af-
> ter a sharp reversal in the condition of a man being kept alive by
> the only mechanical heart of its kind.**

When a listener hears that question before he hears what happened, does
he have the slightest idea what the anchor's talking about? Better:

> **The first man with the so-called Penn State heart has taken a bad
> turn, and his doctors are trying to find out what went wrong.**

Who needs rhetorical questions like this one:

When did NASA know about problems with the shuttle's rocket boosters, and what did the agency do about it?

Why not skip the questions and go straight to the news? Better:

The commission on the *Challenger* explosion will try to find out today when NASA learned about problems with the shuttle's rocket boosters. And what the agency did about them.

Question: What did the French president and the prime minister know and when did they know it?

Dear anchor, don't you think listeners can recognize a question by the word order and the rising inflection? And can do it without being told they're about to be asked a question? Isn't there a better way to start this story than with a question, a question that echoes one first asked during Watergate, one that through overuse has become waterlogged? Another usage that has become soggy:

Smith's throwing arm is the big *question mark*.

Should a nurse be paid as much as a prison guard? That's the contention of the American Nurses Association. . . .

Should a writer be paid for turning out that *non sequitur?* How can anyone contend a question?

Here's a riddle: What totally American art form has been overhauled by some people in Argentina who want to bring it back home to America right after they market-test it in France?

A riddle? "Market-test" or "test-market"? (Do you "drive-test" a car or "test-drive" it?)

Of course, they play the same courses, they use basically the same equipment, but how different is women's golf, that is, big-time women's golf from men's golf? We're going to be putting that question to two of the very best women on the golf tour in just a few minutes.

Didn't the anchor consider the peril of a premature pronoun *(they),* one that precedes the subject? In this case, the peril is more pronounced because the anchor never does say who *they* are. And the opening *of course* is way off course. That's no way to start a story or an intro. As for the question, if I were to ask an audience, that isn't the way I'd put it—or putt it.

What looks like a large potato and travels at high speeds?

A promo for *M*A*S*H?* The newscaster's answer to his half-baked question: Halley's comet.

Is it good news or bad news: the falling dollar and the rising yen?

True or false: The newscaster was writing under the influence of Sam Goldwyn, who reportedly said, "For your information, I would like to ask a question."

What's wrong with question leads? When was the last time you started a conversation with a question? (Except for "How are you?") And when was the last time you bought a newspaper to read its questions? Or turned on a newscast to catch the latest questions?

Any other reasons those leads are objectionable? Yes; they don't inform and don't get to the point pronto.

So why do writers persist in whipping up question leads? Is it because they don't know the answers? Or because it's easier to ask a question than to burrow through a jumble of facts and think through a newsy lead?

Is a question lead ever acceptable? Perhaps, if the anchor is not playing games with the listener and the question is either one that a listener can answer, almost instantly, or one that provokes thought—but not too much thought, lest the listener lose the thread. In almost all cases, though, answers beat questions. No question about it.

3.15 Starting stories with pre-fabricated phrases.

Don't. One of the most common pre-fabs is "In a surprise move," as in this lead from a network broadcast:

In a surprise move, the Interstate Commerce Commission rejected the proposal to merge the Santa Fe and Southern Pacific railroads.

I had long forgotten about the proposal. The ICC had been considering it for two and a half years. So how could I be surprised about the decision when I wasn't aware it was pending? For whom was the rejection a surprise? People in the transportation industry, perhaps. But for the rest of us, news is full of surprises.

Among the most frazzled of pre-fabricated phrases are these:

> This is the story of. . . .
> It's official. . . .
> Once upon a time. . . .
> Now it can be told. . . .
> It shouldn't come as any surprise. . . .
> It had to happen eventually. . . .
> Mayor Mozzarella made it official today. . . .
> The mayor fired the opening shot today in the. . . .
> When was the last time you . . . .
> Believe it or not!
> [Lebanon] is no stranger to violence.
> [Orville Oliver] is no stranger to politics.
> For City Hall today, it was the best of times, it was the worst of times.
> It was business as usual today at. . . .
> What we know now is. . . .
> It's that time of year again.
> Here we go again.

Most of these word packets are the kinds secretaries can type on a word processor with one keystroke, like "In response to your letter" and "Very truly yours." Lawyers call these groupings "boilerplate," strips of words that are extruded into contracts automatically with little thought or effort.

Here are some other pre-fabs that creep—or leap—into broadcast news leads:

> At a hastily called news conference. . . .
> At a crowded news conference. . . .
> In a prepared statement. . . .
> In a bloodless, pre-dawn coup. . . .
> In an abrupt about-face. . . .
> None the worse for wear. . . .

Makes an editor want to weep.

3.16 Scaring listeners.

Don't. And don't scare them away. A prime—but not prime-time—example is this first sentence of a broadcast script:

This is a very complicated and confusing financial story.

Why start with a turnoff? No matter how complex or confusing the story, our job is to simplify and clarify, not scarify. We're often faced with stories that seem impenetrable. But we need to get a grip on ourselves—and on our notes or source copy—and plow ahead. And not tell our listeners that we're baffled or buffaloed (even if we are). "The world doesn't want to hear about labor pains," the pitcher Johnny Sain said, "it only wants to see the baby."

That scare was probably not intentional; we certainly don't want one that is:

How does the thought of 10 percent ground bones and other meat remnants in hot dogs, sausage or bologna sound to you?

I'd tell the weenie who wrote that, "Don't try to upset me or my stomach. And please don't question me."

Many scripts are scary for another reason: they've been put on the air apparently untouched by human hand—or mind.

There are many ways to rob a lead of its clarity and impact besides the 16 ways listed above. You can probably think of other ways, or catch some the next time you listen to a newscast.

When you're writing a lead, remember you're writing the most important sentence in your script. So avoid the Lead Writer's Deadly Don'ts. You'll be rewarded with listeners and viewers who are with you right out of the starting blocks, who stay with you until the end of the newscast, and who come back tomorrow.

4

FINE POINTS/FINE POINTERS

*Press on: Nothing in the world will take the place of
perseverance. Talent will not; nothing is more common than
unsuccessful men with talent. Genius will not; unrewarded genius is
almost a proverb. Education will not; the world is full of educated
derelicts. Persistence and determination alone are omnipotent.*

Calvin Coolidge

By now, you probably have realized that the best way to deliver news stories to your listeners is to write the way you talk. (And you're probably starting to notice flawed newswriting when you hear it on the air.) But several refinements can help make your writing (and maybe your talking) even more effective. Let's call them Fine Points/Fine Pointers.

Incorporate these tips into your copy and you'll set yourself apart from lazy writers who don't pay attention to details, or don't know which details they should be paying attention to. If you follow these tips, your listeners will get more from your newscasts—without even realizing why.

4.1 Avoid *may, might, could, should, seems* in your first sentence.

They're linking verbs, but they're even wimpier than *is:* they wobble. And they waffle. They don't say anything for sure. Whenever possible, make a definite statement, not one that has the ring of *maybe yes, maybe no.* Can you imagine a strong script that starts with a sentence riding on *seems?* That's even weaker than *is.* At least, *is* says something is. *Seems* says only that it *may* be. So another word to avoid in a lead is *may.* Even softer is the verb *might,* which in the present tense *(might* is also the past tense of *may)* indicates a possibility that is even less likely than *may.*

If the facts of the story suggest that something may occur, I think through the lead carefully to try to find a way to say something definite.

Instead of saying,

The space shuttle *Pegasus* may finally get off the ground today.

I'd say,

The space shuttle *Pegasus* will try again today to get off the ground.

The second lead may be only marginally better, but at least it has more strength than the one with *may,* which carries the implied burden of *may not.*

4.2 Use connectives—*and, also, but, so, because*—to link sentences.

Connectives join sentences and allow listeners to see how they're tied together in one fabric. Using connectives makes it easier to follow the thread.

No matter what your sixth-grade teacher might have told you, feel free to start a sentence with a connective. Example: "Mayor Collins was indicted today. A grand jury charged him with grand larceny—stealing more than 10-thousand dollars from petty cash. *Because* of the indictment, the mayor said, he's taking indefinite leave." *Because* connects that sentence to the one before. And *indictment* also helps the listener even though *indicted* was used in the first sentence.

4.3 Use possessives—*his, her, its, their*—to tie sentences and facts together.

Instead of talking about "the car," you can make it "*her* car. " If you think listeners would have any doubt about who *he, she* or *it* refers to, don't hesitate to repeat the noun itself: "The car crashed into a home, and *its* roof caved in." The antecedent of *its* is home, but some listeners might take it to mean that it was the *car* whose roof caved in. To remove all doubt, delete *its* and substitute *the home's.* Although we have to be frugal in using words, don't fret about repeating a word to make sure a sentence is clear. You have to write not only so that you're understood but also so that you're not misunderstood.

4.4 Use contractions—with caution.

Contractions are conversational and time-savers. But some contractions can cause confusion; the most common hazard is *can't*. Even careful listeners—and they're not plentiful—often miss the final *'t*. So they think they hear *can,* contrary to what the story is trying to stress: can*not*. So we run the risk of confusing listeners when we use a negative contraction if the loss of the final letter(s) leaves only the positive form. But some contractions are safe to use even if a newscaster swallows the final *'t* or a listener has a hearing problem: among them, *don't, won't*. Even if a listener misses the final *'t,* he's not going to mistake the sound of *don't* (dough) with do (due).

4.5 Pep up your copy with words like *new, now, but, says.*

Not only does *new* signal a listener that he's hearing news, but it can also compress a mouthful into one short word.

Instead of writing,

The government issued a report today that says. . . . ,

we can start speedily,

A new report says. . . .

Now has two good uses: it shows that an event is going on at this very moment, and it indicates a reversal in course. For example:

Sheriff Gooch has denied he was on duty when. . . . But *now* he says. . . .

4.6 Put the word or words you want to emphasize at the end of your sentence.

Try to construct periodic sentences. A periodic sentence creates tension, interest and emphasis as it goes along by placing the most important word or words at the end. So don't take the edge off by ending a sentence with weak, incidental or irrelevant words.

One expert says books about writing have not given the element of emphasis enough emphasis. According to Theodore A. Rees Cheney in *Getting the Words Right,* "A word or idea gains emphasis (and is therefore remembered) if it is positioned right before the period that ends the sentence. . . ." The type of sentence suggested by Cheney builds tension and suspense by saving its impact or meaning until the end. F. L. Lucas writes in *Style,* "The most emphatic place in clause or sentence is the end. This is the climax; and during the momentary pause that follows, that last word continues, as it were, to reverberate. . . . It has, in fact, the last word."

In *The Elements of Style,* Strunk and White also tell us how to deal with emphasis: "The proper place in the sentence for the word or group of words that the writer desires to make most prominent is usually the end."

And David Lambuth says in *The Golden Book on Writing:* "Unless you have good reason for doing otherwise, put your most important word or phrase at the end of the sentence. The most important word is usually a substantive [a word or group of words having the same function as a noun] or verb. Don't sacrifice the strategic final position to a preposition or even to an adverb, unless it really is the most significant word—which it sometimes is. The well-known advice against ending a sentence with a preposition is valid only [with] unimportant prepositions. In certain cases, a preposition is the most emphatic word to end a sentence with."

In contrast to the periodic sentence, the cumulative (or loose) sentence makes a statement and keeps on going, adding subordinate elements, like modifiers, clauses and phrases, as it rolls all over the place, which is what this sentence is doing before your very eyes, accumulating more add-ons. It could have ended after any of the last few commas.

"There is a slackness to a loose sentence, a lack of tension," Thomas Whissen says in *A Way with Words.* He calls it comfortable and easy to write. But he observes, "There is no real build-up, no anticipation, no excitement."

A contemporary expert, Bryan A. Garner, writes in *The Elements of Legal Style:* "It is only a slight exaggeration to say that a 'sentence must be so written that the punch word comes at the end.' That the end is emphatic explains why periodic sentences work."

One of the benefits of the periodic sentence is that it builds up to the main point. Unlike the loose sentence, it doesn't make its point and then run downhill. As Lambuth writes, "Build *up* to your big idea, not *down* from it."

Most sentences in newspapers and wire copy are loose. And most of us, when chatting, use loose sentences. If we had time to think through our thoughts thoroughly, we'd use far more periodic sentences. They carry the most impact and are the most rememberable.

Bell Labs has found that people remember best what they hear last, so if you want your words to sink in and to be remembered, use periodic sentences. Not exclusively, but frequently.

Let's see how to transform leads that rely on loose sentences to leads that put the emphasis at the end of the sentence, where it usually belongs. Here's a lead from a network newscast:

> **Matters went from bad to worse between the United States and Libya today.**

The point of that story is the slide from bad to worse. But the point lies in the middle of that excerpt, which means it's buried. That's the worst place to put the most important fact. And yes, *today* is in an awkward place. Better:

> **Relations between this country and Libya have gone from bad to worse.**

Here's another network example that needs restructuring:

> **Union Carbide said today that *equipment trouble and workers who didn't know what they were doing* were to blame for this month's chemical leak at the company's Institute, West Virginia, plant that sent more than a hundred people to the hospital.**

That's some sentence! Not a good one, but a long, busy and confusing one. Imagine trying to read that on air. Imagine listening to it. Imagine trying to understand it.

I've italicized the key fact—-the cause of the leak. Or, at least, what the owner says is the cause. And that key fact shouldn't be submerged in the middle of that marsh. As it's written, the most memorable part of the sentence focuses on the people hospitalized, a fact reported previously— many times. Now let's apply the principles of emphasis to improve that sentence:

> **Union Carbide says the leak at its plant in Institute, West Virginia, was caused by equipment trouble and workers who didn't know what they were doing.**

The original sentence was 41 words; the rewrite, 26 words. Shorter, sharper, stronger.

4.7 Watch out for *I, we, our, here, up, down.*

When *I* is used in a direct quotation in a story, it's open to misunderstanding:

The mayor said, "I need to take off weight."

The listener has good reason to believe the mayor is referring to the anchor. So paraphrase:

The mayor said he needs to take off weight.

And I'm also puzzled when a newscaster uses *we.* Is the newscaster using *we* to avoid *I?* When she says *we,* is she referring to her newsroom, her community, or what? *Our* is too possessive unless you're writing about something that is yours, something that belongs to you or your station. Avoid "*our* troops" unless your station maintains its own militia. As newspeople, we report from the sidelines, not as partisans or participants.

Here should almost always be deleted from copy. *Here* causes the listener to wonder whether the speaker means "here in our newsroom" or "here in our town." Newscasters also start stories like this: "*Here* in Hicksville. . . ." Hicksvilleans know they're in Hicksville. They don't need to be reminded.

Up and *down,* as directions, are objectionable for similar reasons. In conversation, when talking about the town to our north, we'd say "*up* in Hangtown." When writing for broadcast, don't say "*up* in Hangtown." For folks north of Hangtown, Hangtown is *down.* Another adverb to watch for is *out,* as in "*Out* in Far Corners." People out there regard themselves as insiders. In their worldview, every place else is *out.*

4.8 Wipe out *ing* spots.

If you keep hearing an *ing*ing in your ears, it may be because some newscasts carry more *ings* than buses in Beijing (where the common family name of Ng is usually pronounced by Americans as *ing*). Here's an example:

> *Raising* clenched fists and *singing* freedom songs, 20-thousand blacks are *gathering* for a mass funeral in a segregated South African township. Police are out in force, but there has been no trouble. Twenty-nine victims of racial unrest are *being* buried.

That network story is weaker than a sapling. Instead of telling us at the outset who or what the story is about, the writer starts with a participial phrase and slides in low gear to another participle. That conceals the subject and leaves us baffled.

The weakness of the first sentence in the story is compounded by the lack of a finite verb, one with a tense. The second sentence is weak because it rests on *are* and *has been,* both forms of a linking verb, *to be. Are* is in the active voice but expresses no action, so it's static.

In the second sentence of the story, *but* is incorrect. *But* implies that what is to follow changes course or is contrary to what might be expected. If police are plentiful, I wouldn't expect trouble. It might be more logical to write, "Police are out in force, *so* there has been no trouble." But I wouldn't use *so* because we can't know for sure why there has been no trouble.

The third sentence of the story refers to "victims of racial unrest." This is delusive. Unrest does not kill.

That sentence also says the victims "are *being* buried" as though it's being done now. Yet the first sentence tells us that people are *raising fists, singing* songs and *gathering* for the funeral. All four of those activities cannot be going on simultaneously.

Let's assume the victims were "*going* to be buried" and rewrite the opening:

> A mass funeral in South Africa has drawn a vast crowd, 20-thousand blacks. As they gathered for the burial of 29 blacks killed in riots (?), the mourners sang freedom songs and raised their fists.

Now let's look at another network weakling that's also annoying: it bounces from *ing* to *ing* like the cartoon character Gerald McBoing-Boing:

> A U.S. Supreme Court *ruling* today that could affect millions of workers nationwide, a *ruling* that states may force employers to provide particular kinds of benefits in their company insurance plans, for instance, *requiring* mental health, alcohol or drug abuse services.

The subject—a ruling that could affect millions—is not followed by a verb. An incomplete sentence works once in a while, but that sentence, which is the entire item, is too long. And confusing.

When you were reading *a ruling that states,* didn't you think for an instant that *states* was a verb?

In that item, the first two *ing* words are nouns, the third is a participle. But whether an *ing* word is a participle (an adjectival form derived from a verb), a gerund (a nounlike form), or a noun, some writers often use them in threes and fours. Here's a script from the Midwest:

> **U.S. Agriculture Secretary Richard Lyng spent the *morning* in Buffalo County, *eating* breakfast in Gibbon and *talking* with community leaders there and *visiting* two Buffalo County farms.**

Is there something in a writer's first *ing* that triggers a mechanism in his mind that sends a stream of *ings* flowing into his copy? Just asking.

This script comes from elsewhere:

> **President Reagan and his wife, Nancy, are *continuing* their August vacation in southern California, but correspondent ___ ____ *is saying* the president and his wife are *taking* a break from the routine of the presidential ranch near Santa Barbara.**

News reflects change, so I keep saying that *continues* or *continuing* is an unsatisfactory word to use in a lead because it tells the listener that whatever has been going on is still going on.

That lead-in implies that the correspondent is going around saying something. And saying it and saying it. And in the next lead-in, the same writer keeps doing it:

> **Big-city mayors from across the country are *meeting* in New York City *talking* about *drug-trafficking.* And correspondent ____ _____ *is saying* a great deal of attention is being paid to the latest drug fad, the *smoking* of crack.**

One possible explanation for writers' *ing*ing is that they want to tell listeners that events are going on at this very moment, even as we're speaking, and they think *ing* imparts immediacy. An occasional *ing* may add zing, but a cluster can cloy. And can make a story soft, ungrammatical, illogical, or false.

One of the most disagreeable of all *ings* is the mistaken use of a participle as the main verb in a sentence, as in this network lead-in:

Japan's transport minister today *ordering* inspections of all Boeing 747s now in use in the country.

On the same newscast on the same day, another leaden lead-in:

Pope John Paul *continuing* his visit to Africa with a stopover in Zaire.

Here are a couple of other examples, made up by Cameron Knowles of WSGW-AM, Saginaw, Michigan:

President Clinton and Russian President Yeltsin signing an important trade deal today. The president saying it's a good deal for the U-S and Russia. . . .

British Prime Minister John Major deciding to talk to the I-R-A. Opposition leaders calling the move a disaster. . . .

Knowles says: "I think the writers are trying to eliminate the use of the conjugated form of the verb 'to be'—*is, are,* et cetera. I think the use is grammatically incorrect."

Not only ungrammatical, but also unnatural, unconversational, unjournalistic and unjustifiable. Literate adults don't talk like that. Literate children don't, either. But toddlers learning to talk, do talk like that: "Mommy going out?" And Mommy or Daddy might reply: "Yes, mommy *is* going out." Without thinking about it, a grownup speaks correctly by inserting *is.* Unless that grownup lapses into baby-talk.

If you take the subway in New York City, you can hear people *ing*-ing in the train: "My brother going to that game." When people speak that way, you figure they're new to our country and haven't learned basic English yet. Or else they're school drop-outs—or push-outs.

Literate speakers of English aren't always able to recite the rules of grammar, or parse a sentence (let alone diagram one), or explain why they say what they say the way they say it. But they know, almost instinctively, from speaking English all their lives, from hearing it spoken, from going to school, and from reading books, magazines and newspapers, they know that those examples offered by Cameron are wrong.

In the first example, *signing,* a participle with no helping verb (like *is*) in front of it is an adjective. A verb has three basic tenses: past, present and future. Tense tells us whether an action has already taken place, is now taking place, or will be taking place. If the first example had used *signed,* or *is signing,* or *will sign,* it would help clue in the listener.

A participle is called a verbal, but it's not a verb. So the sentence fragments in Cameron's examples lack the one element that has the power to drive a sentence: a verb. No one can make a sentence go without a verb. No one. Not Hercules, not Houdini, not even Hillary.

Some listeners would assume *signing* in the example is the start of an adjectival phrase set off by commas, and they'd wait for the sentence to be completed by what grammarians call the predicate—and what Paul Niwa of CNBC calls the meat and potatoes. Perhaps those listeners would expect the sentence to end like this: "agreed to meet again tomorrow." Yet the way that example is written, listeners haven't the slightest clue whether the two presidents have already signed, are signing this very moment, or will be signing.

So let's supply verbs and convert those examples into sentences that make sense:

> **President Clinton and Russian President Yeltsin signed an important trade deal today. Mister Clinton says it's a good deal for the United States and Russia.**

We should be aware that we need a *where* soon and insert the name of the place where the signing occurred. But at least we've translated that example from *Ing*lish into English. Now let's do the same for the second example: "British Prime Minister John Major has decided to talk to the I-R-A. But opposition leaders call the move a disaster."

The spread of the *ing* thing is what the grammarian H. W. Fowler might have called the survival of the unfittest. What impels writers to *ing* it? Probably a feeling that it makes news sound more newsy, more streamlined, more even-as-I-speak. But as we can see and hear (from the *ing*ing in our ears), *ing* is the wrong thing.

4.9 Don't create *ize* spots.

They can pop up in your copy right before your eyes. I heard this one myself: A network newscaster said diplomats had worked out an agreement and had "initialized" it. *Initialized?* The suffix *ize* has long been fused onto nouns and adjectives to turn them into verbs: *apologize, burglarize, computerize, hospitalize, jeopardize, legalize, pasteurize, polarize, synthesize,* even *decriminalize.* I won't itemize them, but writers should realize they can't slap on an *ize* indiscriminately, especially if an existing verb does the job. "Initialize" is not needed because an established verb, *to initial,* already means "to sign one's initials."

A community newspaper in St. Louis told of someone who had been "funeralized." And a local newscaster spoke of "unionized" teachers. This usage seems strange; it made me think of teachers who had been processed in some way—but not quite funeralized.

Another misbegotten verb is *finalize.* It has the ring, or thud, of bureaucratic jargon, and we already have ways to convey the action intended by *finalize:* "end," "make final," "put in final form," "finish," "complete," "wrap up." Under *finalize,* the *American Heritage Dictionary* (1992) says the verb "is frequently associated with the language of bureaucracy and so is objected to by many writers." And the *AHD* says *finalize* was unacceptable to 71 percent of its usage panel. But the 1969 *AHD* reported *finalize* was found unacceptable by 90 percent of the panel; so opposition to *finalize* has slipped about one percentage point a year. The final word isn't in yet, so let's wait till the fat lady croaks.

4.10 Don't be an adjective-stacker.

Another problem I don't sympathize with or temporize about: what some grammarians call "stacking." That's the practice of piling adjectives and nouns-as-adjectives in front of nouns. One of the most horrendous examples was uncorked by a network newscaster who spoke of **"a new and improved revised downward federal budget deficit forecast."**

Rather than punctuate that, I'll puncture it. When the anchor reaches the first noun, *budget,* the average listener probably thinks that's the subject of the sentence. But it's quickly followed by another noun, *deficit,* so he realigns his train of thought, if he can, and surmises that the story is about a budget deficit. Wrong. All those adjectives and nouns modify what it's really all about: a *forecast.*

A listener can catch a couple of adjectives before a noun, but seven adjectives are far too many, especially those seven. What makes it even tougher to untangle is that two of them *(budget, deficit)* are nouns pressed into service as adjectives. The sentence should be rewritten—and the writer sentenced.

A newspaper *reader* might be able to thread his way through that terrible thicket of words because he'd first see the headline, read the sentence at his own pace, reread whatever isn't clear and then perhaps rip it out of the paper for another read-through. Any story written that heavy-handedly ought to be ripped out—and up. But a *listener* who wanted to figure out that sentence as it was spoken would have had to be a Champollion (the French Egyptologist who deciphered the Rosetta Stone). Or have total recall—with instant replay.

The problem with that kind of over-writing is that a listener can't grasp it instantly. The problem with that writer was not that he wasn't trying. He was trying too hard. Maybe he wanted to make himself heard by hammering out a punchy sentence, one that would put a dent in the listener's mind. But no one will ever remember it, and children will never recite it. And that's *my* forecast.

4.11 Don't characterize news as *good, bad, shocking* or *interesting.*

Just report the news. Let the listener decide whether it's good, bad or interesting. What is good for some is bad for others. What seems, at first glance, to be good, can turn out bad.

What's good for a city dweller may be bad for a farmer. What's good for Luke Skywalker may be bad for Lucy Streetwalker. Bad news for Main Street is often good news for Wall Street. The plunge in oil prices seemed like good news, but in many places in this country, it turned out to be bad news. Heavy rain can be bad for pedestrians, motorists and sunbathers. But it can be good for farmers, taxi drivers and umbrella vendors.

"Good news" abounds on broadcasts when the prime rate drops. But for listeners, a drop in the prime has both positive and negative sides. Anyone who takes out a home improvement loan, for example, will benefit right away. And if other borrowing costs start to fall again, consumers could save interest on adjustable rate home mortgages and similar borrowings.

But for many listeners, lower rates are "bad news." Many consumers like high interest rates because it enables them to earn strong returns on their investments, like money market funds and U.S. government securities.

I also was taught not to tell an audience that a story is distressing, or interesting, or amusing; let *listeners* decide. The best policy is to stick to the facts and just tell the news.

Even more undesirable for newswriters—but not necessarily for comedians—is the good news-bad news combo:

Governor Gibson had good news and bad news today. He said he's going to push for a tax cut—but not this year.

What makes it objectionable is that it has become tattered. In fact, the "good news-bad news" gimmick has been traced back to Biblical times. When Moses came down from Mount Sinai with the Commandments, he reportedly told his people, "I have good news and bad news. The good news is that I got them down from 40 to 10. The bad news is that adultery is still in."

I said "reportedly" because a news director who reads that may muse, "If a minicam wasn't there to shoot it, did it really happen?"

I do think it's unobjectionable to use the "good news" approach when the news is indisputably good for a specific group or person:

The I-R-S had good news today for taxpayers.

Governor Boodle received good news and bad news today. His good news: he was put on probation. His bad news: he has to make restitution.

Otherwise, the time-consuming, subjective "good news" label is bad news. And please don't call a story "unusual." We don't report the usual, do we? Not usually.

4.12 Dump *details.*

Avoid the word *details.* In my book, *details* is a dirty word. Certainly, writers should have an eye for detail. And know when and how to present a *telling* detail—yet not tell many details. And not call them *details.*

When I hear the word *details,* I think of the tiny print in a lease or a contract, the specs for a stereo component, or something else where I don't want to get bogged down with details. I assume that most listeners regard *details* with a similar lack of interest. Yet anchors often introduce reporters this way: "Sally Golightly has the details." Better: "Sally Golightly has the story." Or a "Sally Golightly reports." Or "Sally Golightly reports that [provide a fact from her script]." Or say it some other way. Just don't bother me with *details.*

4.13 Handle quotations properly.

Quoth a network newscaster:

Gorbachev delivered his sharpest attack yet against President Reagan's 'Star Wars' plan, warning of, quote, 'rough times ahead' if President Reagan and his aides, quote, 'continue along the perilous path they have laid.' Unquote.

To *quote* or not to *quote?* That is the question: whether 'tis nobler in the mind to *quote* or take another tack to avoid a sea of troubles.

That and other quotidian questions about quotations vex many a writer, so let's see what experts say. And let's start with one of the earliest efforts to quash *quote:* "Thoughtless use of such hackneyed terms as 'quote' and 'end quote' tend to interrupt the listener's thought. They have a barking, staccato sound no matter how softly they are spoken. They call attention to themselves and detract from the story." The criticism comes from *A Manual of Radio News Writing* by Burton L. Hotaling, published in 1947.

Another expert on the same wavelength was the first news director of CBS, Paul W. White. He wrote in *News on the Air,* also published in 1947: "Remember that since the word 'quote' is foreign to the ear as far as ordinary conversation is concerned, it probably always is disturbing to the listener. . . . Please, please don't use 'unquote.'"

"Such phrases as 'and I quote' and 'end quote' are . . . shunned by skillful writers," Mitchell V. Charnley said in *News by Radio,* published in 1948. "The need for them can be avoided in most cases by careful use of the more conversational devices." (Until 1947, Charnley said, publications on handling radio news were scant: apparently only two mimeographed handbooks printed before World War II and two pamphlets issued by news agencies during the war.)

"Avoid the words 'quote,' 'unquote' and 'end quote. . . .' This style has become trite and stilted." 1947. Baskett Mosse, *Radio News Handbook.* He said that more than a half century ago.

"It is old-fashioned to say 'quote' and 'unquote.'" 1967. *Broadcast Writing Style Guide,* U.S. Defense Information School.

More often than not, says the 1972 *AP Broadcast News Style Book* using direct quotations in stories is "lazy writing."

"The oldtime use of quote-unquote has long gone by the boards. . . ." 1976. *The Associated Press Broadcast News Style Book.*

"Don't use the hackneyed QUOTE-UNQUOTE." 1982. E. Joseph Broussard and Jack F. Holgate, *Writing and Reporting Broadcast News.*

"Never use the words *quote, unquote* and *quotation.*" 1982. Frederick Shook and Dan Lattimore, *The Broadcast News Process.*

"The use of the terms 'quote' and 'unquote' is cumbersome and lacks finesse." 1984. J. Clark Weaver, *Broadcast Newswriting as Process.*

"You should avoid using the expression 'quote . . . unquote.' 1984. Ted White, Adrian J. Meppen and Steve Young, *Broadcast News Writing, Reporting, and Production.*

"Avoid the use of 'quote-unquote.'" 1986. Mark W. Hall, *Broadcast Journalism.*

"Do not EVER say 'quote' and 'unquote.' That is a holdover from the ancient days of sending news by telegraph when the sending operator wanted to be certain the receiving end knew the limits of the quoted material." 1987. R. H. MacDonald, *A Broadcast News Manual of Style.*

"These words [*quote* and *unquote*] are jarring to the ear; they are abrupt and interrupt the flow of the story. Rather than clarifying, they may well confuse the listener. Even more stiff and formal are the phrases: 'and I quote' and 'end of quote.'" 1988. Roger L. Walters, *Broadcast Writing.*

The same disdain for *quote* and *unquote* is also expressed in the most recent books. *Broadcast News,* 3d edition, published in 1993, says, "This heavy-handed device [*quote*] has become antiquated." The author, Mitchell Stephens, suggests the use of "more subtle and less formal alternatives."

These attributing phrases inform listeners in a conversational way that they're about to hear a direct quotation:

He put it this way. . . .

In her words. . . .

The governor's exact words were. . . .

As he put it. . . .

. . . what she called. . . .

These are the mayor's words. . . .

In other words, there are many other words. Yet some writers use *quote* and *unquote* so often you'd think they're trying to fill a quota. Maybe they need to consider a few more quotations:

"NEVER use the old 'quote, unquote' method." 1993. K. Tim Wulfemeyer, *Beginning Broadcast Newswriting,* 3d ed.

"It is awkward and unnecessary to start and end a quotation with the verbal quotation marks *quote* and *unquote.*" 1994. Edward Bliss Jr. and James L. Hoyt, *Writing News for Broadcast,* 3d edition.

"Do not use phrases like *quote* and *end quote* or *unquote.*" 1996. Peter E. Mayeux, *Broadcast News Writing & Reporting.*

When should a writer use a direct quotation? "Only when it's neat, compact and the wording is exceptional," says Mitch Stephens. "Otherwise, paraphrase."

In *Crafting the News for Electronic Media,* Carl Hausman says, "You do not read 'quote' and 'close quote' or similar indicators over the air, except when the quote is of such a controversial or bizarre nature that you want to ensure that listeners or viewers completely understand that these are the newsmaker's words and not yours." One such extraordinary remark could be handled this way: "President Nixon said, *quote-,* 'I am not a crook,' *unquote.*" If you wrote, "President Nixon says he's not a crook," you'd drain the remark of its tang.

So let's rewrite what the newscaster said in the excerpt at the outset of this section:

> **Gorbachev made his sharpest attack yet on President Reagan's 'Star Wars' plan. He warned of** [here the newscaster can pause or punctuate with his voice] **'rough times ahead' if President Reagan and his aides continue on what he called their 'perilous path.'**

And now if you need help in your newsroom to give *quote-unquote* its quietus, you can quote our quorum.

4.14 Don't end stories with pre-fabricated phrases.

This is the flip side of the advice in chapter 3 about avoiding pre-fabs in your leads. Ending a story with a pre-fabricated phrase is just as bad.

Some to shun:

> Police are investigating. (Since when is that news?)
> What happens next remains to be seen.
> Only time will tell.
> Now the ball is in the mayor's court.
> Don't count him out yet.
> As Yogi Berra put it, "It ain't over till it's over."
> It'll probably get worse before it gets better.
> The full story is yet to be told.
> In the final analysis.
> No one knows what the outcome will be.

The final chapter is yet to be written.
There's no end in sight.

And variations without end.

4.15 Don't overuse *today* and *tonight*.

Every day, newswriters wonder where in a story to insert *today*—or whether to put it in at all. Even when placed properly, a string of *todays* can daze listeners, with *today, today, today* tapping a tatoo on their tympani. (Ditto, *tonight.*)

"In the broadcasting business," Allan Jackson of CBS News once wrote, "the customers (your listeners) assume you're talking about what happened today; in fact, by the very nature of the medium, they assume you're talking about what is happening not only today but, to a large extent, right now. Allan died more than twenty years ago, but his advice is timeless.

The first editor of the *CBS Evening News with Walter Cronkite,* Ed Bliss, told me that his chief chore in scrutinizing the scripts of the three writers was deleting *today*. Although Ed was jesting, he made it clear that the overuse of *today* is nothing to wink at. Using *today* in the first story of a newscast seems reasonable, maybe in the first two stories. But in his *Writing News for Broadcast,* Ed advises, "Avoid a succession of leads containing the word *today*, especially in news summaries when repetition of the word becomes painful."

"It is a mark of the amateur to use *today* in every story you write," according to another textbook, *Broadcast News Writing, Reporting and Production* by Ted White, Adrian J. Meppen and Steve Young. "Your listeners," they write, "assume that your stories deal with events that are taking place today without your reminding them every 20 seconds."

On evening newscasts, *this evening* or *tonight* in a story may make a script seem newsier. But some stations, in an effort to make their late newscasts seem different from their evening news and more up-to-the-minute, put *tonight* in every story. So even if a story is fresh or has a new angle, this approach palls.

For example, an anchor on a late newscast reported, "A British researcher said tonight. . . ." That was the first time I ever heard of a researcher who made public his findings just before dawn, as it was in Britain—unless he called a news conference for 1 a.m.

When we talk about the time and *today* and *tonight,* we should use our local time. Occasionally, a writer will see a wire story from Moscow that says the Kremlin said something *tonight.* The time in Moscow when the Kremlin spoke might have been 7 p.m. But in Washington, D.C., that's mid-morning. Yet, a few U.S. newscasters will go on the air at 6 p.m. or later and say, "Moscow said *tonight*. . . ." I'd say the person who writes it that way is either thoughtless or careless with the truth.

A careful writer would make his script read, "Moscow said *today*. . . ." But in most cases, the writer could skip the time element and use the present tense: "Moscow *says*. . . ." The illogic of using any but local time is apparent in this imaginary lead: "A top Russian official said *tomorrow*. . . ." Only infrequently is it necessary to say that it's *tomorrow* in Moscow and that something occurred at dawn there.

If a story—or a producer—does cry out for a *today* or a *tonight,* where in a sentence do we put that adverb? If you use *today* or *tonight* in the first sentence, use it *after* the verb. It makes no sense to use *today* before the verb, before we even tell listeners what the action is.

We hear stories that start, "The White House today said. . . ." The use of today near the top delays listeners from learning why they should keep listening. If you must use *today* in a story like that, you can make it, "The White House said today. . . ."

Today is one of those words so commonplace in newscasts that they induce yawns, according to Mitchell Stephens in *Broadcast News.* "They are best kept out of the lead," he writes, "or at least out of the first few words of the lead—what might be called the 'lead's lead.' News is what is special about a story, not what is common to every story."

Avoid putting *today* at the end of the first sentence unless it's especially short. Putting *today* at the end can be awkward and make the story wrong. Yet I heard this on a network newscast:

Another Lebanese died of injuries received in that terrorist bombing of the U-S embassy today.

Sounds like the bomb went off today; but no, the Lebanese *died* today.

As for starting a story with *today* or *tonight,* don't, unless it's intended as a transition from a closely related story with a different time element. Another possible exception: to draw a sharp contrast, perhaps something like this:

Today, Mayor Meyer passed a tough physical. Tonight, he dropped dead.

But I'd probably write it this way:

Mayor Meyer is dead. He died tonight of. . . .

Another angle on *today* comes from the newsman Jerry Bohnen, who says he tries to avoid *today.* He says *today* is too broad and covers too great a time span. Instead, he prefers to "narrow the time frame" for the listener. Rather than say, "A judge will decide *today,*" Jerry favors saying, "A judge will decide *this afternoon.*" Although that's longer than a simple *today,* it is more specific and more immediate. If you have time, his approach may occasionally be appropriate. On an evening newscast, though, I wouldn't say that something happened *this morning.* That's too long ago, too long to say, and immaterial. Nor, on an evening newscast, would I say that something happened *this afternoon.* It's wordy and immaterial. *Today* would suffice.

In most cases, it's unimportant whether the mayor said something at 10:30 a.m. or 4:30 p.m. But if the story just broke and the news is significant, I might consider featuring the time element:

Mayor Trumbull says he's resigning. *A few minutes ago,* he said his doctor advised him to move promptly to a warmer climate.

Or:

Mayor Trumbull is planning to resign *within the hour.*

Or:

Mayor Trumbull and Governor Graham are meeting *now.*

I think those words, where appropriate, heighten the now-ness of news.

Not so in the case of the word *tonight.* Night after night, newscasters start stories with *tonight* and pepper story after story with *tonight.* So many *tonights* are sprinkled in newscasts you'd think some stations were plugging a new product named Tonite. Intended as a stimulant, it's now a depressant.

The writers' intentions are good: they want to make their late newscasts differ from their early 'casts. To do that, some writers try to find out what's new so they can update the story. Some writers, though, re-use the early script word for word. Or merely re-word it. Naughty, naughty! They shouldn't take a script from an earlier newscast and re-use it or use it as the basis for a rewrite. If the story is good enough to be broadcast again, you should get the original source material (perhaps wire copy) and work from that. But freshen it. And tell it in your own words.

The reason you shouldn't rewrite an earlier script: the writer, even you, might have left out or downplayed something worthwhile. Or taken the wrong tack. Or made a factual error. So don't risk perpetuating that first script's error(s). Start anew. And make it new. News, as you know, is what's new.

Many writers who retell stories broadcast earlier think the best way to go is to insert *tonight.* Some writers go through such contortions to stress *tonight* that they twist their sentences out of shape. And when writers inject *tonight* into certain stories, they also twist the truth.

Let's look at several broadcast examples:

Two top school officials in Du Page County tonight are pleading not guilty to charges they used school funds to pay for activities at sex clubs.

Where are they pleading, in night court? They almost certainly entered their plea that day, not at night. So the use of the present progressive tense, *are pleading,* which stresses the continuity of the action, is suspect. Further, the adverb *tonight* (or *today*) is best placed after the verb. The script would have been strengthened by making it *"their* activities." I assume they're charged with spending the school's money on their own activities.

In Chicago politics tonight, the mayor and his city council opponents are locking horns once again. Aldermen from the council's majority bloc forced adjournment of today's council meeting, just 23 minutes after it began.

In the first place, the "in" lead is weak, the word *politics* a waste. (Who'd ever start a story about the president by saying, "In national government tonight"?) In the second place, if the meeting broke up hours ago, during the day, how could they still be locking horns *tonight?* If you keep seasoning your scripts with contrived *tonight*s, how do you point up the freshness of a genuinely new story that *did* break tonight?

And *locking horns* should be consigned to the cliché closet, unless you're writing about trombonists at a jam session. As for that unnatural *tonight,* let's respect our listeners' intelligence and not try to hornswoggle them.

In DeKalb County tonight, just outside the town of Somonauk, the search goes on tonight for a seven-year-old girl.

That was the lead story, so one *tonight* might be all right, but two in one sentence? After all, listeners know that *are still searching* has to be *now, right now, at this very moment,* and they also know that when it's 10 p.m. and dark outside, they're engulfed by night. So they don't need to be reminded repeatedly.

The first four words of the script hold no attraction for listeners. Starting with *in* is pointless. And there's no reason to turn a good verb like *search* into a noun. And no need for *the town of.* Also, *outside* can be reduced to *near.* Better: "Police and volunteers in DeKalb County are still searching near Somonauk for a seven-year-old girl."

Here's a network script:

Actor Stacy Keach is a free man tonight. Keach was released from a prison in England this morning after serving six months of a nine-month sentence for smuggling cocaine.

On a 10 p.m. or 11 p.m. newscast, why mention *this morning* unless the time element is significant?

If you're trying to avoid *today* in the first sentence of a script in the belief that *today* sounds too long ago, use the present perfect tense. It shows an action has been perfected, or completed, at the time of writing or speaking but is still pertinent; it can also show that an action is continuing into the present. Use of the present perfect tense also enables you to avoid that dirty word *yesterday* in the lead.

4.16 Avoid meaningless transitions.

Transitions should be unnoticeable. A skillful cabinetmaker joins his panels neatly. Leaving the joints exposed is considered poor craftsmanship, and Ron Meador says bridging them with crude or clumsy devices "is like assembling fine furniture with roofing nails."

One of most over-used transitions is *meanwhile*—as in "*Meanwhile*, the White House said it's studying the problem." I hesitate to say there's never an occasion to use *meanwhile*. But I've never run across it—except right here. Use of *meanwhile* to tie two items together shows listeners the stitches. By directing attention to itself, *meanwhile* gives away our m.o. Another reason a careful writer avoids *meanwhile:* other careful writers have told him to. Also, it evokes facetious undertones, as in the pornographer's "Meanwhile, back at the raunch."

The BBC stylebook calls *meanwhile* "a lazy link word that is almost always redundant." *Meanwhile* means "at the same time" or "in the intervening time;" even more meaningless is *in the meanwhile.* Also avoid *meantime,* unless you're writing about G.M.T.—Greenwich Mean Time.

When you need a transition from one story to a closely related story, you can start the second item with a dateline:

In Washington, the White House says it's studying the problem.

(If a horse can talk, why not a house?)

Or link the second story by starting with a time-element like *tomorrow.* Or *later.* Or find a fact in the second story that makes the two stories related and slip that fact into your first sentence to serve as a bridge. Or link the items with *and* or *but:*

***And* the city council also voted to turn Main Street into a pedestrian mall.**

Or:

***But* the city council rejected the mayor's proposal. . . .**

Whatever you decide, don't use *on another front* as a transition, unless you're writing about a war with several fronts—or a weather front. Also, avoid using *closer to home* as a transition. Sometimes we hear that after a foreign story. Yet the new story often turns out to be nowhere near where we are. But don't use *elsewhere;* everywhere is elsewhere.

Don't use *in other news* as a transition. Every story on a newscast is other news. Each story differs from all other stories. If the first five minutes of your newscast has been devoted to one big story, shift to the next story by going to a commercial. Or pausing. Or changing tone. Or changing camera. Or anchor. Or writer.

According to an able transition team, Arthur Wimer and Dale Brix, the best transitions are word bridges. At least when they seem helpful and logical and the words aren't wasted. "Otherwise," they say in their *Workbook for Radio and TV News Editing and Writing,* "don't use [transitions] if they seem forced, illogical or awkward."

After many a tragedy, we hear this transition: *on a lighter note,* which implies that what we just heard was light and what we're going to hear is even lighter. After a tragedy, anything is lighter, including a lesser tragedy. After a bombing, a local anchor said,

On a much lighter note. . . .

And a network anchor said:

Health officials today raised the number of known Ebola patients in Zaire to 114, with 79 dead. On a much lighter note from the world of micro-bugs, there is word tonight of a remarkable achievement.

On a heavier note: please weigh your words.

Speaking of strained segues—and that's another type of transition to trash—this was broadcast on a New York City TV station: After an anchor described John Glenn (erroneously) as "the first man to orbit the earth" (he was the first *American*), his co-anchor said,

And speaking of the earth, the earth has weather, and here's our weatherman.

And speaking of weathermen, they, too, can chill me. A weatherman on another New York City station said, "We're sitting under a convective flow." Huh? What's that? And a Los Angeles meteorologist reported "a split flow in the 500-millibar chart," whatever that is. Made me think of splitting for Malabar. Or Malibu. But let's not use as a transition that old Monty Python line: "And now for something completely different."

Many news directors will tell you that finding a good writer is hard. But if you follow the tips set down in chapters 1, 2 and 3, you can become a good newswriter, or at least a better one. And even better than most of the hordes of applicants competing for newsroom jobs. Sad to say, in a way, if you follow the tips in this chapter, you can be a better writer than many of the people who already have jobs in newsrooms—even big-time newsrooms. So don't settle for becoming just adequate. Aim higher. Be the best you can be.

5

PUTTING IT ALL TOGETHER

*You're supposed to describe things
in terms that make sense to the truck driver
without insulting the intelligence of the professor.*
Edward R. Murrow

You've learned the basics of broadcast news writing, studied the style tips and practiced them. You can write a sentence so it sounds conversational and slides easily into the ear. You're not wasting words. And you know how to write an engaging lead. Now it's time to fit sentences together into stories.

Much of what goes on the air comes from wire services. Small-market stations with small news staffs—or no news staff—often "rip and read" wire copy. But newswriters in bigger newsrooms spend a lot of time rewriting stories transmitted by the news services or sent by other sources.

Rewriting wire copy is excellent practice. It requires all the skills broadcast newswriters must employ, even when writing a script that's based on their own reporting. You need to take a large amount of information and condense it into a short story for broadcast. You need to make decisions, sometimes tough ones, about which facts to include and which to exclude. You need to determine the essence of the story and put it into a lead sentence that captures your listeners' attention and draws them into the story. And you need to use all the rules and tools of the broadcast writer to carry your listeners with you to the end. And on to the next story. And you must do it under the pressure of deadlines that arrive too soon.

So here are some tips on how to do all that. They grow out of my experience as a writer (and a rewriter), and from the experiences of others who have put in their time at the keyboard, staring blankly, with the producer shouting across the newsroom, "Well, where is it?" or " I need it *now!*"

5.1 Read—and understand—your source copy.

Read it to the end. Carefully. Don't write a script after reading only two or three paragraphs of the source copy. If you don't understand something, don't use it. Because, if *you* don't understand it, how can you write it so that your listeners understand? Too many writers lift words and phrases from source copy and transplant them into their own copy without knowing what they mean. When an editor or producer asks what something in the script means, many a writer replies, "Well, that's what the wire copy says." Don't be a copycat.

5.2 Underline or circle key facts.

By marking your source copy—preferably with a red or orange pen—you'll see instantly what's important and what you should consider including in your script. This can be a big help in boiling down the important and interesting to the essential. Your markings will also help when you check those facts in your completed script against your source material. You can make your mark by circling, underlining or highlighting.

As you develop your news judgment, you'll do a better job deciding which facts to use and in which order. And which facts to omit. The more you learn about what makes news, the better you'll be able to write news. So it helps to ponder the question "What is news?" One of the best answers is provided by an authority on journalism, Melvin Mencher. He says: "Most news stories (1) are about events that have an **impact** on many people, (2) describe **unusual** or exceptional situations or events, or (3) are about widely known or **prominent** people." In *Basic Media Writing,* he goes on to say that other elements heighten the news value of an event, including **conflict, proximity** and **timeliness.** "Boiled down to its essentials," Mencher says, "every story is about either a **person** who has said or done something important or interesting or a **person** to whom something important or interesting has happened." Or the story is about "an **event** of importance or interest to many people."

5.3 Don't write yet.

Think. Don't just do something; sit there. And think. Allow time for incubation and meditation. Not much time, but some. Even if you're fighting the clock, you may be able to take as much as 30 seconds. And if you're working on a script for tomorrow, you can afford more than that.

I once had a producer who often snapped: "Write. Don't think." (He became a network vice president.) Unless you're up against a deadline, with no time to spare, take time to think. Even if it's for only 30 seconds, think: think what the story is all about; think what the heart of the news is; think of the best way to tell it. Think.

5.4 Start strong. Well begun is half done.

The most important words you'll write in a story are those that come first, what Mitchell Stephens calls (in *Broadcast News*) "the lead's lead." So bear down on your first sentence. "Start strong" doesn't mean to make the story stronger than the facts warrant; and it doesn't mean to exaggerate or misrepresent. But it does mean to put all your mental power into the start. Your first words are very likely to determine whether your listeners keep listening. So focus on your first words and your first sentence. If you set sail with even a small compass error and if it's uncorrected, you can wind up way off course, even on the rocks, or at the bottom. As Euripides once told me, a bad beginning makes a bad ending.

5.5 Apply the rules for broadcast newswriting.

Our source copy doesn't play by these rules. Wire copy for newspapers generally crams the five W's—*who, what, when, where* and *why*—and *how* into the first paragraph or two. And for good reason: when a newspaper sets a story into type and it's too long for the allotted space on the page layout, an editor is most likely to trim from the bottom, often lopping off entire paragraphs. Because most wire service reporters come from newspapers, they stick with that form of writing.

Another reason newspaper people put the best first is that if they're writing against a deadline, they don't know whether they'll be able to get more than a few paragraphs into the next edition. They figure they'd better jam their best material into the lead. They set down facts in descending order of importance, writing in a pattern known as the inverted pyramid. So newspaper reporters develop the habit of front-loading, putting all the best material at the top. And they write the most expendable material last.

But we broadcast writers don't usually have room for the five W's and *how.* And how we don't! So we ignore the inverted pyramid. But we can't ignore the flaws of some wire copy written in wirese or journalese. Journalese is defined in *Webster's Unabridged Dictionary,* 2d edition, as "writing marked by triteness, oversimplification, verbal distortion, unwarranted exaggeration, and coloring for persuasive or sensational effect."

Journalese is a quaint tongue we have to translate into basic English while we write. As newspaper style developed over the centuries, it deviated further and further from the way people speak. Read a newspaper or wire service lead aloud and you'll be reminded how different they are from us, how print style doesn't suit our broadcast needs. That's why we've developed our own broadcast style, a style geared to a receiver far different from the eye: the ear.

People who read newspapers can give them their full attention. They read whatever they wish and at their own speed. And they can reread and mull over whatever interests them. Listeners can't do that with broadcast stories, so we must adjust our language to allow for the peculiarities of their hearing apparatus, which processes information relatively slowly. That's why we must make our copy simple and direct.

An approach for this kind of lean, clean, clear writing is sketched by Strunk and White: "Vigorous writing is concise. A sentence should contain no unnecessary words, a paragraph no unnecessary sentences, for the same reason that a drawing should have no unnecessary lines and a machine no unnecessary parts. This requires not that the writer make all his sentences short, or that he avoid all detail and treat his subjects only in outline, but that every word tell."

Set your mental processor to adjust every sentence until it conforms with broadcast rules. Writers who have mastered the rules know that rules help make their writing work right. Yet, the ultimate test for any kind of writing isn't whether it follows all the rules but whether it works.

5.6 Develop the courage—and the competence and the confidence—to write simply.

How simply? Don't worry, we're not writing for simpletons. But we are writing for a general audience, comprising listeners at all levels of interest, knowledge and brainpower. Which means we would do well to heed David Lambuth's advice in *The Golden Book on Writing:* "Don't try to seem learned or literary by using long or unfamiliar words. . . . As far as possible, a writer should write in the very words he does his thinking. These are usually simple, homely words. . . . The best rule for writing—as well as for speaking—is to use always the simplest words that will accurately convey your thought."

5.7 Refrain from wordy warm-ups.

Get to the point. But what if you don't get the point or don't even see the point? If you've read the source copy, marked it, thought it through and are still stumped, put your source copy face down and tell the story to your keyboard in your own words. If you do that without glancing at the source copy, you'll probably confine yourself to the highlights, which is just what you're supposed to do. Don't fret about producing perfect copy; just get it down in rough form. You may not be sure what you want to say until you see what you've said. Read your script and re-read it. Delete any unnecessary words. If you don't need to keep them in, you do need to keep them out.

If that approach doesn't work, pretend you're telling the story to a friend by phone. Let's say your friend is out of town and you're out of pocket. You wouldn't rattle on. You wouldn't digress or say any more than it takes for your friend to get the gist. You'd tell your story hurriedly, and you'd hit only the high points. You wouldn't talk in the curt style of a nine-word telegram (isn't the tenth word usually *love*?). You'd speak in a conversational style. So once you delete the unnecessary words, you'll have your lead. Or at least a good framework for your script.

If you find that that doesn't do the trick, try to visualize tomorrow morning's newspaper and its front page: how would the banner stretching across the top of the page capsulize the story? Which few words would a headline writer choose to condense a complex event? When you put your mind to it, you can often get a handle on a story that way.

If a gas tank blows up and kills 50 people, a newspaper headline might read,

50 DIE IN BLAST

But for us, in broadcast news, even after filling in that scanty line with verbs, articles and a few facts—**Fifty people are dead in the explo-**

sion of a gas tank in Hackville—the result is unsuitable. As soon as you say 50 people *are* dead, the story starts sliding downhill. It's best to set the scene first and tell what happened. *Are* is weak, as is any form of *to be; explosion* obscures *explodes;* and the place-name is mentioned last, so the listener doesn't have the slightest idea where the explosion happened until the end of the sentence.

The newspaper banner offers only the bare bones. You need to take that skeleton and flesh it out to get a sentence in broadcast style:

A gas tank in Hackville blew up today and killed 50 people.

Why didn't I write "blew up today, *killing* 50 people"? Because a finite verb, one with a tense *(killed),* is stronger than a participle *(killing)* with its *ing* ending. *Died* is best used for people who died of natural causes.

The second sentence of a script usually answers questions raised by the first: how many people were hurt? What caused the explosion? Did the victims work at the gas storage depot? Were any homes damaged? What is the impact on Hackville?

Too many questions to be answered in one sentence. So the third sentence answers questions raised by the second sentence as well as any other unanswered questions. And the fourth sentence, if your story runs that long, answers questions not answered by the third sentence. Ideally, your sentences hold hands: they flow smoothly and seamlessly. And listeners aren't aware of your hard work and careful construction.

When I'm stumped in deciding what a story is all about, I use the technique I just laid out: I try to picture the front page of tomorrow morning's newspaper. Some newswriters begin by shutting their eyes; some stare into space, as if they expect to see cue cards; some hop right to it and bat out a story one, two, three. Some imagine the event in their mind's eye. The mind's eye can see plenty: from a nuclear explosion to a sunset in Sarasota. The best way is the one that works for you. If you haven't found your way, keep at it anyway.

5.8 Omit needless words. (Thank you, Strunk and White.)

Try to rid your copy of *that*s, *which*es, *who is*es, *of*s and other space-eaters. As you read your script, you may spot a few space-eaters sneaking in. In most cases, they can be deleted with no loss of meaning—and with a gain in clarity. One reason to rid your copy of needless words is that they lengthen your sentences and force your listeners to work to extract the substance. Bear in mind: if you say what needs to be said, the fewer words you use to tell a story, the clearer and more forceful your script

The importance of examining the need for every word is pointed up in a joke told by Harold Evans in *Newsman's English:* A London fish-monger had a sign that said: **FRESH FISH SOLD HERE.** A friend per-suaded him to rub out the word FRESH; he wasn't expected to sell fish that wasn't fresh. Then the friend persuaded him to rub out HERE; he's selling it, naturally, in his shop. Then the friend urged him to rub out SOLD; he isn't expected to give it away. Finally, the friend persuaded him to rub out FISH; you can smell it a mile off.

5.9 Hit only the main points; trash the trivia.

Because the wires carry something doesn't mean we should use it. Some wire service reporters write long because they haven't learned to write short. Some write long because newspapers have plenty of space to fill and some shovel in wire copy by the yard But *we* have to be highly se-lective. The minutiae that a newspaper might print are, for us, useless.

Don't cram too much information into a story. Too many facts, too many names, too many numbers, too many words are too much for lis-teners. They just can't process a steady flow of facts. Brinkley has said the ear is "the worst, least effective way to absorb information." (*David* Brink-ley, not Christie.) No matter how complex the story, our job is to compress the facts and give the listener not just the essence but a highly concen-trated essence: the quintessence. Architect Ludwig Mies van der Rohe, a minimalist, used to say, "Less is more." His critics retorted (not in uni-son), "Less is less." And I say, "More is less." Moreover, more is a bore. See to it that every word you use is indispensable and that you use noth-ing that's superfluous. Whatever you say, say only once. Life is too short for any repetition, except my suggestions.

5.10 Don't parrot source copy.

When a wire story has a clever play on words, or an unusual combi-nation of words, avoid borrowing that language. Why? Because if we do borrow, a listener who recalls hearing the same words on an earlier news-cast on another station may say, "So that's where that jerk gets his news!"

Even though broadcast wires are supposed to be written for the ear to accommodate subscribers, the quality of the copy is uneven. Not all of it is written by people who are adept or experienced. Why parrot what *any* writer has said? Aren't you a better writer? Or trying to be one? We should rewrite wire stories using our own words and phrasing.

5.11 Humanize your copy.

Write about *people,* not about *personnel.*

Whoever wrote this wire service story should be reported to the Missing People's Bureau:

> **Tribal factions angered over a beer hall dispute fought with sticks and iron bars Sunday at Kloof gold mine west of Johannesburg, killing seven black miners and badly injuring 39, police said.**

For use on the air, this "A" wire story needs major surgery. "Faction" is an abstraction, so we shouldn't write about factions fighting. Our listeners can't see factions, but they can see people. So we should talk about members of tribes, or blacks, or black tribesmen. And, as you know by now, we don't put attribution at the end of a sentence.

Another type of story that often needs people-izing is a statistical release. Instead of borrowing references to "a decline in births," we should, where possible, write about "fewer babies." Instead of writing about "unemployment," we should, where time and context permit, talk about "people out of work." Instead of talking about "deaths,"we should, where appropriate, talk about "*people* killed" or "*people* who died."

People want to hear about people. Abstractions don't breathe—or bleed. Besides humanizing stories, we should also be on the alert to localize them, to bring a national story down to a local level, to report its local effects.

5.12 When in doubt, leave it out.

Go with what you know. Just before airtime, when we handle so much copy, we probably can't find answers to all our questions about the source material, or resolve ambiguities, or reconcile discrepancies. Yet we can't assume. Or speculate. We deal only in facts, not in conjecture. The wires are not infallible. Far from it. Their stories are gathered, written and edited not by superhumans but by imperfect humans like us. (Isn't *that* a scary thought!)

You must be even more careful if your source copy is a press release. Wire service stories are written by newspeople who work for news agencies; in effect, they work for us. They're hired for journalistic skills. And they're trained to report objectively. But press agents aren't journalists. They're not disinterested parties. And they don't work for us. They work for someone else. Their silent slogan is, "Whose bread I eat, his song I sing."

Whether they call themselves press agents, press information officers or public relations counselors, they still work for private parties. And, as the adage has it, "Who pays the piper calls the tune." With few exceptions, they are not paid for their objectivity, devotion to the public weal and dedication to Truth. The press releases they write, which they often label *news* releases, are written for the benefit of their private interests, not our public interests. Sometimes their interests and ours intersect, and we find a release worth using. But that release may or may not be accurate. It may or may not be complete. It may or may not be fair.

If you decide to use a press release or a part of one, rewrite it. But first, make sure that the person named as the sender did in fact send it, that it's not a hoax. Even if it's not a hoax, remember that the release comes from someone who is, in effect, a salesman, trying to "sell" you a story, one written to advance his interests, not necessarily yours.

If you doubt any key points in the release, pick up your phone and verify them on your own. If you can't verify them but decide to go ahead anyway, be sure to attribute them to someone named in the release. Many press agents are honorable people, and they write releases that are reliable. But some press agents slip in a few curves. It's your job to detect them—and reject them. "The most essential gift for a good writer," as Hemingway put it so elegantly, "is a built-in shockproof shit-detector."

Another source of problems—and opportunities—is telephone tips. People phone newsrooms with all sorts of motives: some callers are looking for kicks, some for rewards, some for vengeance. Any caller can identify himself as just about anyone else. Listen carefully, ask questions and treat each call as potentially newsworthy. But when you hang up, don't go straight to your keyboard. Verify everything you want to use. But don't try to verify a tip simply by phoning the tipster and talking to him again.

Some pranksters delight in phoning in obituaries. Never use an obit before first checking with the undertaker. And watch out for mischief-makers. I remember a cub reporter who was refused service by a Chicago nightclub because he wasn't wearing a tie. So he walked across the street to a saloon, where a TV set was carrying a telethon. In a twinkling, he got an inspiration. He phoned the telethon and said he was the manager of the nightclub that had denied him service and wanted to make a contribution to fight some dreaded disease: $5. The TV host's on-air announcement of the measly gift made the famous club look like a den of Scrooges, and the reporter got his revenge. Yes, I did. (Thinking about it makes me want to hum "Pranks for the Memory.")

Yet, you shouldn't take my cautionary words as advice to hang up on unfamiliar or anonymous callers. Or to ignore them. Or to make prank calls of your own. Another Chicago reporter, Martin J. O'Connor, used to say he didn't care if a tip came from Judas Iscariot. If Marty could confirm it, he'd run with it. Once you have confirmed a story, it's yours.

5.13 Don't raise questions you don't answer.

Don't insert a fact that cries out for clarification. Not long ago, I read a script about a fire in a trailer park. The script said a man was killed in a trailer, "where he lived with a companion." But no one told us whether the companion survived, nor whether the companion was a colleen or a collie.

5.14 Don't use newspaper constructions.

This is an example of a common newspaper construction:

The chairman of the Senate Foreign Relations Committee said today Moscow should stop threatening Washington. Senator John Walton said. . . .

Most newspaper readers would probably see that Walton is the person described in the first sentence, the committee chairman. But in broadcasting, the nature of the medium leads many listeners to assume that the Walton in the second sentence is someone else and that Walton is adding his voice to the chairman's. In broadcasting, it's better to write,

The chairman of the Senate Foreign Relations Committee, John Walton, said today. . . . .

Or:

The chairman of the Senate Foreign Relations Committee said today. . . . Chairman John Walton told. . . .

That makes Walton's identity unmistakable.

For writers with a newspaper background, a reminder: don't write in the inverted-pyramid style described in paragraph 5.5 of this chapter. Leave that to newspaper people.

In journalism school, I was taught in a class in broadcast newswriting not to use newspaper terms. After it sank in, it struck me as reasonable. Why should we, in a far different medium, use lingo devised for another medium, one that broadcasting tries to be different from? Yet I hear newscasters refer to people or stories "in the headlines." What headlines? Are they plugging newspapers? And some newscasters talk about their "front page," their "sports page," their "people page," their "back page," even their "cover story." "Cover" for TV? Yep, and they aren't referring to dust covers. Another publishing word borrowed by broadcasters is "magazine." It's also a place of storage and a storehouse of information, so perhaps its use in broadcasting can be justified. But "pages"? The only pages I know in broadcasting run errands.

5.15 Read your copy aloud. If it sounds like writing, rewrite it.

What counts is not how it looks on paper but how it sounds. If it sounds un-conversational, as though written for the eye, rewrite it. When you read it aloud, you might also catch any unfortunate sequence of words. For example, a BBC news reader (as the Beeb calls anchors) said, so the story goes, that in a golf match Lord Hampton "had been playing a round" with Lady Fairfax. If the reader had read his script aloud, he might have caught that double meaning. I'm not saying a writer should have a dirty mind, but it helps. And it also helps to have a mind that's nimble enough to catch single words that seem safe on paper but can lead to complications. For example: "query." You may never be tempted to use "dastard," but be careful of "duck" and "finger" (as verbs), "shift," "morass," "horticulture" and "Uranus."

The broadcaster who wrote this news item also should have listened to his script:

> **An Interior Department report on Teton Dam is still pending. So are congressional studies of the Bureau of Reclamation and other dam-building agencies.**

The writer should have caught "dam-building agencies." The listener can't see the hyphen, so the phrase sounds like a curse. If you read your script aloud to yourself before turning it in, you'll catch seemingly innocent combinations of words that sound damning.

5.16 Rewrite. The art of writing lies in rewriting what you've already rewritten.

True, broadcast writers barely have time to write, let alone rewrite. But when you do have time, or can make time, rewriting usually improves your scripts.

How can writers find time to rewrite? One way is to start writing earlier. Or curtail or rearrange other activities. Another way is to avoid dawdling.

Before we rewrite, we should examine our scripts for signs of sloppy—and sleepy—writing. In the pressure-cooker atmosphere of a newsroom, or a classroom, we often put down the first words that come to mind and lapse into constructions and locutions that are weak and wordy. But if we read—and reread, and rethink—our scripts carefully, we can see the soft spots. Some need to be cut out, others need to be fixed. Take time—and make time—to give your script a good going-over. Is every word necessary? The rule: If it's not necessary to leave it in, it *is* necessary to leave it out.

After you trim flab and get rid of any clutter, ask yourself: Are the words right? And in the right order? And does it read right?

Also: Is every bit of information right? Accuracy is essential. Check all names, dates, amounts, facts with the source copy. As one news agency used to say, "Get it first, but first get it right." (The agency had trouble getting it either way—and went the way of all flash.)

Extra time is scarce in newsrooms, particularly as air time approaches. But if you start writing earlier, skip the chitchat and bear down on writing, maybe you can save enough time to rewrite your copy. And re-rewrite it. The importance of rewriting is illustrated in George Plimpton's interview of Hemingway for the *Paris Review:*

P: How much rewriting do you do?

H: It depends. I rewrote the ending of *Farewell to Arms,* the last page of it, thirty-nine times before I was satisfied.

P: Was there some technical problem there? What was it that had stumped you?

H: Getting the words right.

Getting the words right!

But we don't have as much time as a Hemingway. We write in haste but can't revise at leisure. If we're working on a piece that doesn't have to go on the air tonight, we can let our script sit overnight and cool off. The next day, we're refreshed and we can read it as though it's new. And we can go over it energetically. Maybe this time, after another rewrite or two, we can get the words right.

Before we turn in copy, we should ask ourselves at least three questions, according to René J. Cappon, author of *The Associated Press Guide to News Writing:*

Have I said what I meant to say?

Have I put it as concisely as possible?

Have I put things as simply as possible?

5.17 Don't lose a listener, and don't fail to reach one.

The best way to keep a listener is by talking to him, not at him, and by working at it, not by making him do the work. He won't, so you have to. Writing *is* hard work; anyone who says it's easy is someone who hasn't tried it or doesn't know how to do it well. The work of writing, it is said, can be easy only for those who have not learned to write. Telling a long, complex story in 20 seconds is a challenge for any writer. Telling it well is even harder. As Confucius should have said, "Easy writing, hard listening. Hard writing, easy listening."

5.18 Don't make a factual error.

That's the deadliest sin of all. It causes you to lose your credibility. And eventually your audience. Perhaps even your job.

After you read a wire story, or other source copy, or your own notes, you have to apply all these tips instinctively. You can't take time to review each one step by step, like an airline pilot going down his checklist for takeoff. You have to absorb the tips so they become second nature and you're able to apply them on autopilot. Then your scripts will be all set for air.

Let's look at an example. Here's a long wire story loaded with information about an unusual occurence. Obviously, you can't read it all on the air. It would take up too much time in your newscast, and your network audience (see how quickly you've moved to the top?) doesn't need to know—or want to know—every detail. Also, the wire story is written for the eye, not the ear. So your first task is deciding what to put in your script and what you can safely leave out without denying your listeners an essential bit of information.

Here's the story as it arrived from The Associated Press:

> OKLAHOMA CITY (AP) — A prisoner being taken by federal marshals from Alabama to California bolted out of a moving plane's emergency exit after landing on Saturday and fled into the darkness, authorities said.
>
> U.S. Marshal Stuart Earnest said the escapee, 44-year-old Reginald D. Still, was en route from a federal hospital in Talladega, Ala., to Sacramento, Calif., where he was scheduled to go on trial on a charge of interstate transportation of a stolen motor vehicle.
>
> Earnest said the plane contained 44 prisoners when it touched down at Will Rogers World Airport. No other prisoners tried to escape, he said. Still wearing handcuffs and shackles, he leaped out of the plane's emergency exit, onto a wing and then the tarmac as the plane was braking, the marshal said.
>
> One of eight security people on the plane jumped out to chase the escapee, Earnest said. Federal marshals and local, county, and state authorities fanned out across the airport property, southwest of Oklahoma City, in the search.
>
> Prisoners are normally transported by a Boeing 727, but a backup, a Convair 580 propeller, was being used Saturday because the jet was being repaired, authorities said.
>
> The U.S. marshal's service routinely transports prisoners every other day to courts and penitentiaries around the country. The transportation program is based in Oklahoma City, and prisoners on overnight trips often are housed overnight at a federal correctional facility in El Reno, 30 miles west of here.

Here's the way I wrote it:

A plane with federal prisoners was taxiing at an airport near Oklahoma City this evening when a prisoner jumped off and escaped. While the plane was moving down a runway, he bolted through an emergency exit, landed on a wing, leaped to the ground and got away in the darkness, still in handcuffs and shackles. The plane had been taking him to California to stand trial for theft.

If you've found that one easy, you must have done something wrong; if you start your story by saying a prisoner jumped *out* a plane or even *off* a plane, many listeners might think the plane had been aloft. I wanted to make it clear the plane was on the ground, so my story takes a few extra seconds to get to the nub.

My second and third sentences are easy to follow (certainly easier than he was), they're energized by lively verbs, and the sentences flow in one direction. And you can see the action unfold. The last sentence in my script may seem anticlimactic after the exciting escape, but I wanted to let listeners know that the fugitive is not a killer, at least not yet.

■ I didn't use his name because he's a nonentity, and his name means nothing to listeners.

■ I didn't use his age because I thought it wouldn't tell anyone anything; everyone has an age. I would have mentioned the age of the lamster only if he were a youngster or an oldster.

■ I didn't spell out the charge against him because it takes too much time and would be unnecessary.

■ I didn't say "*car* theft" because a "motor vehicle" could be a car, a van or a truck.

■ I didn't tell where the flight originated or its destination because those places don't figure in the story.

■ I didn't identify the plane because it makes no difference whether it's a Convair or an Electra, whether it's a jet or a prop plane, whether it's taking off or landing. Instead, I focused on that minute of high drama and moved in close.

■ I didn't report the number of inmates aboard the plane because the story was about only one. If any other prisoners had tried to escape, I would have said so, but why take time to report what didn't happen? I was pleased to learn that someone has named a "World" airport for Will Rogers, but I didn't mention it lest I run out of time before my story could get off the ground. I'd have preferred to say "tonight," but I didn't know the time of the escape, so I said "this evening." All I knew was that the guy fled into the darkness. The wire copy moved at almost 11 p.m., but that doesn't mean the story just broke. It could have been several hours old.

At a session of my Television Newswriting Workshop (advt.), I passed out copies of that wire story to the news staff of a TV station and asked everyone to rewrite this Saturday story into a 20-second script for use on a late Saturday newscast. Here's the most inventive lead—and keep in mind that the inmate who fled from the plane was charged with theft:

> **When it comes to vehicles, Reginald Still apparently can take them or leave them.**

Clever, eh? But what would you think if you were hearing it for the first time, with no previous knowledge of the episode? The real test is: what's a listener to make of it? It's easy for insiders to get a kick out of that lead because we already know the story. For listeners, though, this is the first exposure. So they can't savor the wordplay about "vehicles" and the inmate's being able to "take them or leave them." Sounds more like a final observation than an introduction, an epilogue rather than a prologue. Further, I wouldn't use the escapee's name so early. In fact, I didn't use it all. Why not? No listener has heard of him, no listener need hear of him. If I hear the name of an unknown in a lead, I assume he's a hometowner. In this case, the last name, Still, might worsen any confusion. "Still" is a an adverb *(yet),* an adjective *(silent)* and common noun *(distillery).*

In case you're wondering how that inventive writer handled the rest of the story, here is his script in its entirety:

> **When it comes to vehicles, Reginald Still apparently can take them or leave them. Still, an inmate being transferred from Alabama to California, tonight bolted out of a moving plane and fled into the darkness. Police said Still was wearing handcuffs and leg irons when he jumped out an emergency exit. The 44-year-old inmate was scheduled to stand trial on charges of stealing a motor vehicle.**

Sounds as if he leaped from a plane in flight. The script doesn't say whether the plane was aloft or on the ground, just that it was moving. *Tonight* would fit better after *plane*. But one of the most important questions of all: *where* did this happen? No matter what you might think of that lead, the lack of the *where* leaves it nowhere.

How did that writer's deskmates do with the same story? Let's take a look at some of their opening sentences and my brief comments:

It's the stuff movies are made of. . . . a prisoner escape from a moving airplane at an Oklahoma airport.

It's not the stuff good news scripts are made of. Why "movies"? Why not identify the city? Why four periods? Why not a comma or a dash? Why no strong verb, only linking verbs *(is* and *are)* and a verbal *(moving),* which does not behave like a verb? And why turn a good verb, *escape,* into a noun? So that lead gets two thumbs down.

Right now, the manhunt is on for a prisoner who, handcuffed and shackled, lept from a moving plane.

"Right now"? That's no way to start this story—or any story I can think of. By the time this story is broadcast, the fugitive might be recaptured, so the manhunt would be over and "right now" would be wrong now. "*The* manhunt" should be "*a* manhunt." Better yet: "a search." "Lept" (spelled *leapt*) should have been changed to the preferred past tense, "leaped." And there's no *where* there.

Police in Oklahoma City are out chasing their very own Harry Houdini.

Why drag in Houdini? He was a great escape artist, but he died in 1926 and has not reappeared. So now he needs a label: "The master magician Harry Houdini" or something like that. In any case, Houdini has nothing to do with this case. Use of *their very own* makes it sound as if the person they're chasing is a fellow policeman. No, I'm not going to call that story a Houdunit.

A plane left Alabama today carrying 44 prisoners to California. When it got there, it had only 43.

That script is missing a lot more than one prisoner.

Transporting prisoners from one place to another by jet seems to be an escape-proof method. That was until tonight.

Let's not speculate about what *seems* to be. Let's report what we know for sure. Let's tell the news. Now.

Police in Oklahoma City are still looking for a prisoner who jumped out of a moving plane.

"Still looking" makes it seem the escape was reported earlier and that this is a followup. The news is a prisoner's escape. When we talk about someone who jumped out a window, we dispense with *of.* On that basis (a leap of faith?), I'd delete *of* in the script. I'd even take the next step and delete *out.* Instead, I'd write that he "jumped *from* a moving plane."

A federal prisoner, handcuffed and shackled, managed to escape from his captors by jumping from a plane tonight.

Where? Over Alaska? "Managed to escape" = "escaped." "Captors?" A captor is someone who has captured a person or animal. If anything, those marshals are losers.

Federal marshals are wondering tonight how their man got away . . . shackled and in handcuffs.

The writer led with reaction, not action. The news is still the escape. Or Still, the escapee.

Federal marshals in Oklahoma City are looking for an escaped convict.

Again, reaction, not action.

An Alabama prisoner made a daring run for it as he was being flown to California.

A running jump?

Federal marshals in Oklahoma City are hunting for a prisoner who escaped on a wing and a prayer.

He didn't get away on a wing, and he probably was too busy to pray. Which might make this a good place to bail out. Of the dozen or so other scripts on the escape, one or two came close, but I won't inflict any more on you. The writers? All I'll say, to protect the guilty, is that they work in the Lower 48 (states, not markets).

6

LEAD-INS, LEAD-OUTS, VOICE-OVERS

If you write aught, read it through a second time,
for no man can avoid slips. . . . A man's mistakes
in writing bring him into disrepute;
they are remembered against him all his days.
Judah Ibn Tibbon

Now that we've seen how stories can take off, let's see how we can make some other things fly: lead-ins, lead-outs, voice-overs and tease(r)s. The tips and rules that guide us to writing better stories also serve in writing these other elements of a newscast. But each of them has its own peculiar needs.

6.1 Lead-in.

An anchor reads it to lead into a reporter's narrative or a natural sound cut, perhaps of a shouting match. The lead-in sets the scene and identifies the reporter—or the people who are the loud speakers.

The lead-in's job is to alert listeners and prepare them for what's coming—the important, fascinating, exciting, horrifying or amusing story that's about to unfold—but without using any of those adjectives. Yet the lead-in is more than a billboard for the coming attraction. It sets up what follows so it makes sense to a listener. And it supplies a crucial fact or two that may be missing from what follows. Generally, a lead-in should supply the "where." On the other hand, if the reporter immediately says where he is, a lead-in needn't include the "where."

Lead-ins must do more than just lead in. They should keep listeners listening, either through the impact of hard facts told well or through the engaging grace of a light touch. A lead-in should grab a listener by the throat, or by the ears—but gently, politely. Not an easy assignment, especially if the reporter's story is a 97-second weakling. And not if we comply with the truth-in-advertising laws, never promising more in the lead-in than the piece delivers. All we need are the same skills we use in writing "readers" (or "tell" stories)—scripts unaccompanied by footage.

Lead-ins come in many varieties, but, in general, they can be classified as hard or soft. A hard lead-in is usually used to introduce a hard-news story. Ideally, the reporter writes his script as if he were telling the whole story. Then, before the newscast, he gives his first sentence (or two) to the anchor to use as her lead-in. After the anchor goes on air and delivers that lead-in—or a rewrite that retains the essence of the original—the reporter picks up the narrative with the second (or third) sentence of his script. That way, the story flows seamlessly. No maddening repetition, no gaps, no flaps, no traps.

When an anchor doesn't have the benefit of a proposed lead-in from the reporter, the anchor (or writer) should write a lead-in that sets up the story—almost like a newspaper headline. But with sentences that don't sound like headlines or use headline words. If the writer has the opportunity to read the reporter's script in advance, he can include any *essential* facts missing from the script. Or he can give one or two of those facts to the anchor for a tag at the end of the reporter's piece.

A soft lead-in is one usually reserved for soft news. (One kind of lead-in that you don't want to write is *squishy* soft.) Soft lead-ins intro features, human interest and semi-soft stories. Good soft-news lead-ins are hard to write. But, by writing and writing and writing, you can learn to get it right.

As with the Lead Writer's Deadly Don'ts recited earlier in this book, Don'ts are especially important in writing lead-ins:

Don't use the same key words the reporter uses. Don't introduce him or any speaker with the same words he starts with. Violation of that rule produces the "echo-chamber effect." It sounds—and resounds—like this, with the anchor speaking first: "Governor Goober warned today he's fed up with state employees who loaf on the job." Then we hear Goober say: "I'm fed up with state employees who loaf on the job." Or instead, we hear the reporter say, "Goober said he's fed up with state employees who loaf on the job." Listener: "Haven't I heard that somewhere before?"

Or the anchor leads in with something like this: "Old MacDonald said today he's going back to his farm. Steve Simpson reports he's pining for his pigs, ducks and cows." Then Simpson begins, "MacDonald is pining for his pigs, ducks and cows." This leaves the listener higgledy-piggledy, and the duplication wastes time and crowds out other material.

If possible, a writer should prepare a lead-in only after reading the text of the cut or the reporter's script. Or at least talking with the reporter so the writer knows what the reporter is going to say. Or so the reporter knows what the lead-in is going to say.

Don't steal the reporter's thunder. Although the lead-in for a hard-news story should hit one or two highlights, the anchor shouldn't skim off all the good material. Otherwise, the reporter's account will be anticlimactic. It will sound as if the reporter got his news from the anchor. Or, as they say so delicately in the barnyard, the reporter will be left sucking hind teat.

Don't write a soft lead-in for a hard-news story. A soft lead-in may work for a feature story, but a hard-news story calls for a hard-news lead-in. A lead-in is like a store's display window. A dime store doesn't dress a window with diamonds. And a diamond merchant doesn't display dimes. Hard news, like diamonds, deserves an appropriate showcase.

Don't write a lead-in that conflicts with the reporter's script. This may seem abecedarian (no kin to ABC's Sid Darion), but every so often we hear a reporter say something that contradicts what the anchor's lead-in has said. That's a mislead-in.

Don't overstate or oversell. The lead-in shouldn't promise—or suggest— more than the reporter can deliver. It should adhere to standards of journalism, not descend to hucksterism.

Don't be vague. Sometimes, because of the way newscasts are put together, we don't know exactly what the reporter in the field is going to be saying, or which segment of a speech is going to be used. So we have to write "blind"—without saying anything specific. And we put down only enough words to allow the control room to roll tape: "The new chairman of the city transit agency, Lionel Train, spoke out today on the agency's problems." But that's flat. Writing blind, like flying blind, can be risky. Whenever possible, say something substantive: "The new chairman of the city transit agency, Lionel Train, said today he'll clean up the agency's problems within six months."

Don't use a faulty "throw line" at the end of the lead-in to introduce a reporter. You confuse a listener by saying, "Jerry Jarvis has the story" if the next voice we're going to hear is not that of the reporter but of a woman taking an oath of office. One way to handle that "throw line" is to say, "Jerry Jarvis looked on as Mary Barton took the oath."

Most lead-ins run less than 20 seconds, and a few run barely five seconds. No matter what it takes to do the job, no matter what the length, every word counts. And the shorter the lead-in, the greater the need for every word to carry its weight.

6.2 Voice-overs.

If you're in radio, you don't have to worry about V/O's, the scripts that are read over silent videotape. And if you're in TV, you don't have to worry either, as long as you observe these tips:

View the footage before writing. If that seems obvious, think of all the V/O's you've heard on air that didn't fit the picture. If previewing the videotape is out of the question, try to get a shot list (a.k.a., shot sheet, shot card, spot sheet and breakdown sheet). That list itemizes the scenes in chronological order, describes the contents in a few words and provides the running time of each shot as well as the cumulative time. If you do preview the footage, make your own shot list. Without such a list, by the time you get back to your keyboard, you may forget whether the third scene shows injured people or overturned trailer homes, and you may need to know for certain.

Your words don't need to match the picture every step of the way. But they should add to what viewers see—and, if necessary, help them understand what they're seeing. If need be, start to identify the setting and the main characters an instant or two before each new scene comes up. In some pieces, "spotting" a new character—by name or description—is imperative. We call this "keying," "writing to picture" or "cuing words to picture." If we want to write about something the camera didn't shoot or the tape doesn't show but that's pertinent, we "write away from picture."

To help establish what it's all about at the start of a V/O, it's usually best for the script to match the picture. After the viewer is told what it's all about, it may be all right to write away from picture. But don't get carried away. Don't describe in detail what viewers can't see for themselves.

Don't state the obvious. For too many writers, this is not so obvious. That's why we hear lines like "This is the man," "this is the lake," "this is the man jumping into the lake." Viewers can see that. We serve them by supplementing what they see by putting the picture into perspective. We inform them that the water temperature was 35 degrees, that the man weighed 250 pounds and that he didn't know how to swim.

Avoid "Here we see," "shown here" and "seen here." If we're seeing an overturned mobile home, the script needn't whack viewers over the head with a "here." If something needs to be explained or spelled out, do it unobtrusively and without fanfare.

Don't tell viewers to "watch this." If you wish to direct your viewers' attention to something that's about to occur in a long shot, do it subtly. Let's say that in a few seconds a man in the crowd is going to pull a gun and fire. Unless viewers know in advance, they might not be focusing on that part of the screen and could miss the critical part of the action. We can tip them off without issuing orders: "A man on the far right, the man in a khaki jacket, pulls out his gun and prepares to fire at a policeman."

Don't fight picture. Our words shouldn't be at odds with the picture. We shouldn't say zookeepers recaptured two monkeys at the moment viewers see someone holding two children.

Don't use the newspaper phrase "left to right." If several people are on the screen and you need to direct the viewers' attention to someone, you can refer to "the man in the ten-gallon hat" or "the woman with the parasol."

Don't overwrite. Don't squeeze too much copy into the script, making the V/O run longer than the footage. If you have a feature or a soft-news story and don't have to "hit" any scenes, write loose. That way, the words don't overwhelm or drown out the picture.

Don't overload your listeners with facts. Viewers are busy viewing. They're not giving their undivided attention to the words. And too many facts—or words—can cause a sensory overload.

Make use of natural sound and silence. Don't feel obliged to cram words into every single second. If the footage has natural sound, like a gurgling brook, let the picture and sound carry the scene. Even when the footage is silent, you can sometimes skip the narrative. Pause. A few seconds of silence can be eloquent. And, depending on the scene, the anchor's (or reporter's) silence can underline the drama. What kinds of scenes? Perhaps a fireman breathing life into a baby, a lottery winner exploding with joy, a pole vaulter flinging himself over the crossbar.

Be sure the "where" precedes or is at the top of the V/O. If the anchor's lead-in doesn't identify the place, be sure it's identified at the outset in the V/O. Sometimes, though, it's acceptable to identify the place with only a super—the superimposition of characters that spell out the name. Viewers should know right away what they're looking at, where it was shot and when (if it's not fresh).

Read your V/O against the footage while an editor or deskmate watches and listens. This is the best way to catch mistakes and weaknesses. If you time each segment of your copy as you write it, the final run-through should be all right. But don't take any chances: Read your V/O aloud against the footage.

The most frequent weakness in voice-overs written by newcomers, according to Charles F. Cremer, Phillip O. Keirstead and Richard D. Yoakam in *ENG: Television News,* 3d edition, is overwriting. They say the problem is not only that the text exceeds the running time of the video but also that viewers drown in the words and don't get a chance to mesh words and pictures in their minds.

6.3 Tag.

This is the sentence or two that sometimes follow a story or V/O. It's called a tag, cap, button, lead-out or write-out. The tag is supposed to add a bit of information, perhaps an important fact that couldn't be fitted into the lead-in. Or perhaps it's an updated casualty figure. Or late news that should accompany the story just reported. It can be a P.S. that rounds out the story. Or a correction of something that the correspondent had recorded but wasn't edited. Or it might be an anchor's comment or aside. Whatever you call it or whatever you put into it, keep it short and to the point.

Some anchors begin their tags by saying "Incidentally" or "By the way." But it's best to refrain from those transparent efforts to be casual. If an item is indeed incidental, it doesn't deserve valuable air time. And if the item is not incidental, it shouldn't be minimized by being called incidental.

6.4 Tease(r).

A tease is terse. It's designed to inform listeners what lies ahead, to pique their curiosity and tempt them into staying tuned. A tease needs more than compression; it needs crushing. Or squashing. What you might call minimalism to the max. With only several seconds to work in, a writer needs a big vocabulary of short words. Also: creativity, imagination and a discriminating disdain for the rules. Often, there's not enough room for a complete sentence, so she needs to write her line like a headline: "Murder at the Waldorf." Good tease. Lacks a verb but packs a punch.

Yet one of the dangers in condensing a story into a headline is that by reducing and rounding it off, we can easily warp it. And warping can lead to slanting. And distorting. So no matter how catchy the tease you've written, no matter how clever, ask yourself: Is it misleading? Or deceptive? Does it hint of more than the newscast is going to offer? If your answers are no, no, no, then go, go, go.

How often are you annoyed to find that a newspaper headline isn't supported by the story? Often we see that kind of headline in tabloids at supermarket checkout counters. But the headlines are beyond checking out: Siamese Twin Girls Born Pregnant and Man Gives Birth to Test-Tube Twins. Although I haven't heard anything quite that phony in broadcast tease(r)s, I have heard some that flirt with fraud. The kind of tease that brings teases into disrepute is exemplified by "California's on Fire." But California was not on fire. A few hundred acres were on fire. Lesson: Don't get carried away—or *you*'ll get burned.

Apply the same standards to teases that you apply to news stories. We can't always follow writing rules in writing teases, but we must pursue the paramount goal to be fair and factual. We mustn't overstate or over-promise. (Unless we don't mind being the target of a comedy sketch, we shouldn't write a tease that's a parody of itself: "TV teases taken to task. Tape at ten.")

As with any kind of writing or performing, improvement comes through doing it. And doing it. And doing it. And reviewing it.

7

ALL ELSE

*A writer is someone for whom writing is
more difficult than it is for other people.*
Thomas Mann

Q. What else can be said about broadcast newswriting?

A. Plenty else.

Q. O.K., let's start with one else: What are the tricks to writing news?

A. The only trick is to know how to write and to understand what you're writing about. And the secret is to make it seem as if it's not a trick.

Q. Huh?

A. We don't engage in tricks or trickery. The writer H. Jackson Brown, Jr., said: "Don't waste time learning the 'tricks of the trade.' Instead, learn the trade."

Q. But how?

A. They say, "We always learn from others and end up teaching ourselves."

Q. How can you teach yourself?

A. "Teach yourself by your own mistakes," said the novelist William Faulkner. "People learn only by error."

Q. What about shortcuts?

A. There are no shortcuts, no gimmicks, no quick fixes, no simple steps, no easy answers, no magical cures, no cut-rate, can't-miss techniques, no one-fits-all solutions. "There are no shortcuts to any place worth going," according to the singer Beverly Sills. And you can't become a better writer overnight—even if you work the overnight. As a CD developer said, "ROM wasn't built in a day." And as Nero noted, "Rome wasn't burned in a day."

If there ever could be one single answer on how to become a better newswriter, it would be: write, write, write, work, work, work. Work *works*. The more you write, the more you *can* write. The more you can write, the more you can learn. And the better you'll write. As long as you're in class, you're in luck: you have a teacher. But when you start working at a station, you'll need to learn on your own. And also keep learning at your *next* station. (Newspeople aren't stationary; chances are, you'll work at several stations—one at a time.) If you ever consider yourself a finished product, though, you're finished.

Q. I do want to keep learning. And keep earning. But once I leave school, who will be my teacher?

A. Someone who's better.

Q. What if I'm the best in my shop?

A. "Best in my shop" may be only a modest boast: the best may not be much better than the rest. Many newcomers—and old timers—regard themselves as masters. That's why there are so few masters. The critic Robert Hughes said, "The greater the artist the greater the doubt; perfect confidence is granted to the less talented as a consolation prize."

Q. What about getting *outside* help?

A. Most newsrooms don't get outside help. And newspeople, like most other people, find it hard to improve when they have no one to learn from but themselves.

Q. What about learning from writers with more experience?

A. Learn from anyone who knows more than you. The best writers know how much more they have to learn. (At the age of 70, an accomplished French writer said, "Every day I am learning to write.")

Q. So what's the answer?

A. Whether you become a writer or a Writer depends on you.

Q. How so?

A. If you want to improve, and apparently you do, you'll have to do it yourself.

Q. Please explain.

A. Experts say good writing can't be taught but can be learned. I disagree with Oscar Wilde's epigram: "Nothing that is worth knowing can be taught."

Q. What do *you* say?

A. I say writing *can* be taught and *can* be learned.

Q. How?

A. By you, as part-time teacher and full-time learner. The author Jacques Barzun says all good writing is self-taught: "Almost any professional writer will tell you that nobody can teach another person to write. . . . But all writers admit that they were helped by criticism; somebody showed them the effect of what they had written—the unintended bad effect. In doing so, the critic pointed out where the trouble lay and perhaps what its cause was. . . . The truth remains that the would-be writer, using a book or a critic, must teach himself. He must learn to spot his own errors and work out his own ways of removing them." You don't learn from success, you learn from failure—examining failure. The billionaire financier George Soros said: "To others, being wrong is a source of shame; to me, recognizing my mistakes is a source of pride. Once we realize that imperfect understanding is the human condition, there is no shame in being wrong, only in failing to correct our mistakes."

Q. Any other advice?

A. The author John Ciardi says: "A writer can develop only as rapidly as he learns to recognize what is bad in his writing. . . . [The bad writer] never sees what he has actually written. . . . He does not see because, in plain fact, he cares nothing about it. He is out for release, not containment. He is a self-expressor, not a maker. . . ." And as for the good writer: "His progress toward good writing and his recognition of bad writing are bound to unfold at something like the same rate."

Q. Anyone else?

A. For the beginner who asks, "How can I learn to write?" Prof. David L. Grey says the right response is: "Do you care enough to work at it? Or, rephrased: How are your motivation and willingness to accept criticism? Are you willing, literally, to sweat over words? And is your primary purpose random self-expression, or is it to communicate something systematically to someone else? Such a philosophy for writing requires practice and self-discipline, as well as corraling the ego. It demands . . . a willingness to 'grope' relentlessly for the best word and set of words. And it demands active seeking out of the best library and human sources of information and insight."

Q. What else?

A. Listen to the best newscasters and the best reporters, even if it means (sob!) turning to another station or network. Listen carefully. Tape newscasts that have the best writing. Play them back. Replay them. Analyze them. And suss out what makes the best writing the best. But don't try to follow in the footsteps of a writer you admire. "Find your own voice," says the broadcaster Jeff Greenfield. "Don't be Hemingway, Oscar Wilde, Tom Wolfe; they are taken."

Read some of the books on writing mentioned throughout these pages. Read other good books to deepen your appreciation of good writing and to build up the vast fund of general knowledge needed by newswriters. Read widely, read copiously, read unceasingly. You are what you read, so read, read, read.

Keep in mind an observation by the actress Glenda Jackson: "The only lesson you ever learn is how very difficult it is to act well and how very easy it is to act badly." The same is true about writing.

Q. Why haven't you mentioned humor?

A. Funny, thought I had. Humor is hard to write and harder to write about. In news scripts, it's especially fragile. Most news stories don't lend themselves to humor.

Too much of what's intended as humor in newscasts is contrived and clunky. Most often, the best humor in a newscast depends on humorous aspects of the event itself, not in the newswriter's effort to get a laugh. In fact, most real humor in newscasts produces a smile or a glint of appreciation, not a guffaw. We hear too much on the air that's intended to be humorous but sounds as if it has been pounded out with a sledgehammer. What's needed is the delicate touch of a watercolorist.

"Everything is funny as long as it happens to someone else," Will Rogers said. We might have fun *with* someone else, but we never should make fun *of* people. Misfortune isn't a matter for jest. We don't make fun of those who've just lost a game, a home or an election.

One last thought about humor: if you write something that's humorous, don't apologize for it. (That's one of the cynic's four nevers: never complain, never explain, never volunteer, never apologize.) Don't tell your listeners, by word or gesture, that you're uncomfortable with something that's supposed to be humorous. If you're uncomfortable with it, rewrite it. Or, better yet, kill it.

Q. What about puns?

A. As a recovering punster, I'm in no position to puntificate. In scripts, I use them infrequently. They're harder to put across on air than on paper. In print, wordplay sometimes works. But broadcasting is a different playing field. That's because many listeners usually need time to catch on, and we can't call a timeout. A gazette issued by pundits, the *New York Times*'s in-house monitor, "Winners & Sinners," set down two good rules on puns: "If in doubt, don't. If anybody nearby winces, definitely don't." The trouble with so many puns we hear and see is that they're obvious or ham-handed, unless, of course, they're our own. So when in doubt, toss it out.

Q. You haven't mentioned pronunciation.

A. Pronunciation! It's important in broadcasting because mistakes mean a loss in an anchor's (or reporter's) authority and credibility. The columnist Sydney J. Harris says the ten words mispronounced most often are: *nuclear, Realtor, conversant, chaise-longue, harass, lingerie, frequent* (as a verb), *forte, monstrous* and *disastrous.* Several other words that I hear kicked around: *cellulite* (should be pronounced cell-you-light), *covert* (the preferred pronunciation is like *cover* with a final *t*), *dour* (do-er, not dow-er), *lambasting* (as in baste), *onerous* (as in *honor*), *patently* (pay-tently), *schism* (the *sch* is pronounced like *s*), and *long-lived (lived* rhymes with *dived).*

Q. What can be done for writing blocks?

A. For some newswriters, blocks (including this Block) are a recurring problem. A freelance writer sitting at home can afford the luxury of having a writing block. But broadcast newswriters can't. We have to produce a lot of copy in a short time, often in frantic haste. We can't permit ourselves any hangups. So we have to develop inner strength, self-control and devout determination.

If you're stymied by a block and can't get past it, here are several ways to deal with it: do whatever worked for you the last time you were blocked. Or put your story aside—assuming you're not on deadline—and work on something else while your subconscious works on the original story. Or get up and get a cold drink. Or a hot drink. Or eat early. Or walk around in the newsroom. Or leave the newsroom and take a stroll. Or leave the station and take a run. Splash water on your face. Then go back to your original story and get a move on. Discipline yourself. Tell yourself, "I can do it. I will do it. I must do it, I'm going to do it." Then do it. If you're still drawing a blank, think of your paycheck—blank. If that doesn't work, lower your standards. Or run away and join the circus.

Q. How do you deal with the blahs?

A. Don't be blasé. Develop P.M.A. (positive mental attitude). But if newswriting becomes dull for you, if it's no longer interesting or challenging, or never was, maybe you need a change of scenery. Or a new line of work.

Q. How can I learn to write faster?

A. Write more. Speed comes with experience. Meeting deadlines is imperative, but writing fast isn't necessarily a virtue. We're hired as writers, not typists. I can't write without thinking first. So I'm suspicious of speed demons, whose fingers fly across the keyboard. Don't they need time to think? Don't they need time to come up with the right word? Don't they need time to figure out how to say it the best way possible? (Do I sound envious?) Warning: Beware of writers who type faster than they think.

Q. What's the best way to avoid mistakes?

A. Write nothing. Usually, the person who makes no mistakes makes nothing. Mistakes are inevitable when writing in a hurry in the hurly-burly. "The greatest mistake you can make in life," the crackerbarrel philosopher Elbert Hubbard said, "is to be continually fearing you will make one." So don't let anxiety about mistakes spook you. Your goal should be to turn in copy with zero defects. But if writers always succeeded in doing that, editors could be deleted. Writers have someone checking their copy (editors, producers or anchors), but writers still must guard against those pesky errors that try to sneak into copy.

Q. How do you deal with deadlines?

A. Dutifully. How else?

Q. Is there a question you were hoping I'd ask?

A. Yes: "Why bother learning to write well when many superiors, so to speak, don't recognize good writing—and reward bad writing?" My answer is: people who are serious about writing want to write as well as they can. Even the uncommitted don't say, "I want to write just so-so." If you're in the news biz (or any business), you have no business hanging around unless you want to do your best. And who knows? You might wind up working for someone who *does* know—and require—good writing. In any case, why not be the best you can be? If you're content with mediocrity, you've bought, borrowed or boosted the wrong book.

Q. Why did you call this chapter All Else?

A. What else? It's a catchall for odds and ends that didn't fit elsewhere, or that deserved different treatment, or that I forgot to put in earlier.

Q. So why didn't you call it Odds & Ends?

A. I was going to, but then I ran across another book using that title for a chapter.

Q. How did you happen to think of "All Else?"

A. On the "CBS Evening News with Walter Cronkite," the three writers were assigned to stories by category: National, International and All Else. Everything that didn't fit into the first two categories—storms, space, disasters, features, plus the other writers' overflow—went into All Else. As a former All Else writer, I thought it would be an apt heading.

Q. What about "zip?" The title of this book suggests that the book will tell how to write with "zip." Yet you haven't touched on "zip."

A. I might not have been writing with zip, but most of what I've been saying makes for zip. This book's main lesson is that good broadcast newswriting produces copy that's clean, clear and crisp. So if you practice what I've been preaching, you'll write with zip.

Q. Any afterthoughts?

A. Only one thought about "after"—a thought that deserves repeating. If you find "after" in a lead sentence, you should probably rewrite the sentence: put what comes after "after" *before* "after." For instance, you first write, "Police are searching for a man in a Santa Claus suit after he robbed a downtown bank." But then you realize that you've put the cart before the reindeer. So you rewrite it: "A man in a Santa Claus suit has robbed a downtown bank." I wouldn't add "today." If it had occurred yesterday, we would have reported it yesterday. Besides, my use of the present perfect tense—*has robbed*—rules out the need for "today." Also: I wouldn't say the police are searching for him. I probably wouldn't even mention the police, unless they're deliberately *not* searching for him.

Q. Anything else?

A. Yes. If you apply all these tips and rules—and if you apply yourself—*you* can have the last word.

APPENDIX A

Basic Work Rules

These rules are intended to simplify the job of reading a script on the air. They vary from station to station, but the following rules are the most widely accepted:

1. Type a slug—a one- or two-word label for the story—in the upper left hand corner of each page. Type the slug in capital letters. Under the slug, type the date. Under the date, type your last name or initials. A slug looks like this:

FIRE
4/15/99
LCS

Some stations stack those elements, as above; some run them in a single line.

2. Double or triple space all copy.

3. Type your scripts in capitals and lowercase letters, the same style you see in books, newspapers and this style sheet: the first letter in sentences and in proper nouns (names of people, places, etc.) are capitalized; the other letters are lowercase. (Scripts written in all caps are hard to read.)

4. Spell out all words. Don't abbreviate. No symbols: no dollar signs, no parentheses, no percentage signs, no pound signs, no ampersands. But there are a few exceptions: one is *Mrs.* Some newsrooms render Mrs. as *Missus.*

Dates: Add *d, st* or *th:* March 23d (not March 23), March 31st (not March 31), April 15th (not April 15).

Times: Don't spell out A.M. *(ante meridian)* or P.M. *(post meridian).* (Instead of *tomorrow at 10 A-M,* some newsrooms prefer *tomorrow morning at ten o'clock.)*

Years: 19-99, two-thousand.

5. Spell out all numbers from zero through eleven. Spell out fractions: one-third (not 1/3). Write out *hundred, thousand, million.* Write *seven-million dollars,* not *$7,000,000.* And turn *$25,000,000* into *25-million dollars.*

Round off numbers, unless precision is pertinent, as in the rate of inflation: *Inflation rose last month one-point-three percent.* Always spell out *point.* But don't write *15-point-five million dollars;* make it *15 and a half million dollars.* Instead of *eight million, 896-thousand,* write *almost nine million.* And don't start a sentence with figures: Instead of *14 thousand people are at risk,* make it *Fourteen thousand people. . . .* Numbers leave listeners numb. So use numbers sparingly.

6. Use hyphens, as with A-M and P-M, to separate letters that are pronounced individually. Also permissible: F-B-I, C-I-A, Y-M-C-A, N-double-A-C-P and a few others. You can also use initials after you first spell out organizations like the Food and Drug Administration: F-D-A. But acronyms, like NASA, NATO and OPEC, spoken as one word, are spelled all caps with no hyphens.

7. Don't mark up hard copy with newspaper copyediting symbols. If you want to fix a misspelling or insert or transpose a word, black out or strike through the targeted word(s) completely. And above the affected word(s), *print* the change(s) clearly.

8. Provide a pronouncer for a word that's unusual or hard to pronounce. Put the phonetic pronounciation, all caps, in parentheses (yes, they're permissible with pronouncers) right above or right after the word you're focusing on. Right after *Kosciuszko,* add (KOSH-CHOOS-KO).

9. Don't split words between lines or pages. Don't split sentences between pages. If you see that a sentence isn't going to fit at the bottom of the page, start it at the top of the next page.

10. Write only one story on a page.

APPENDIX B

Wire Stories from the CD-ROM

Trifles make perfection, but perfection is no trifle.
Michelangelo

Each wire story offers you an exercise in rewriting. These stories are included on the CD, but you may find it easier to work with this hard copy. Before you rewrite the first story, you'll find it helpful to reread section 5.2 (p. 81) on underlining or circling key facts. And you may find it easier to work by detaching each story from the book and laying it flat on your desk.

Our version of each rewrite and our comments are on the disk—and, we hope, on the mark.

Story 1:

Here's a piece of wire copy. Your assignment: Rewrite it so it becomes a 20-second story for broadcast. Time limit: none. None, because what's paramount here is applying all the tips and rules, not in setting a world indoor speed record.

CHICAGO, August 16 (Reuter) — Binti, an eight-year-old gorilla with a baby of her own, cradled an injured boy in her arms after he fell into the gorilla's concrete enclosure on Friday, a zoo spokeswoman said.

"Binti carried him to a shift door where zookeepers were able to take the child. She exhibited no aggressive behavior," said Sondra Katzen, a spokeswoman for Brookfield Zoo in a Chicago suburb.

Binti was reared by humans and has her own two-year-old baby, the zoo said.

The spokesman said the three-year-old boy managed to climb over a fence guarding the walkway that takes visitors through the zoo's Tropic World, a popular facility that houses several species in addition to gorillas. The boy fell between 15 and 20 feet (4.6 to 6 meters).

Story 2:

Again, make the story for broadcast 20 seconds long. But this time, you have 25 minutes.

San Francisco (UPI) — A huge construction crane tumbled from the 12th story of a new financial district high-rise today, breaking into sections that bounced off neighboring buildings before smashing into rush-hour traffic, killing nine people, authorities said.

Fire chief Fred Postel said five construction workers were believed buried under the debris and listed as missing.

The multi-story crane was being jacked up so construction crews could start work on another floor. Two sections from 75 to 100 feet long snapped off and crashed onto two buses and a taxi on California Street.

At least a dozen people were injured in the 8:15 a.m. mishap, police said.

Police Chief Frank Jordan said nine people were killed.

The falling crane slashed through the top floors of the corrugated metal and girders of a building under construction and being developed by the Federal Home Loan Bank Board. One part banged onto the 10th floor of a neighboring building. Another part glanced off another office building.

The remaining section dangled perilously from the 12th floor, and authorities ordered the evacuation of another 23-story building across the street. Hundreds of people worked there.

A motorized crane was brought to the disaster scene to stabilize the dangling section, police said.

The crashing crane sections struck a San Francisco Unified School District bus and a double-section San Mateo County Transportation District bus.

The Fire Department said the dead included three ironworkers; a woman driving the school bus; a special education student on the school bus and a pedestrian. Jordan said three others also were killed.

The Fire Department said investigators were checking reports the crane operator was trying to pick up a load of metal and was unaware efforts were being made to jack up the crane for work on the next floor.

Bank employee Russ Yarrow said the accident "sounded like the Blue Angels (Navy Precision Flying Team) going over. There was a huge roar or like the sound of a power plant letting off steam—a huge roar just going and going.

"The crane came down and it sheared down through the top five or six floors of the building under construction," he said. "It cut through sheet metal. The girders were bent.

"It looked like a knife cut through butter."

Don Trabert, a stock firm employee in a nearby building, said he looked from his office window and saw two pieces of the crane dangling from the top of the building.

"I just heard a series of bangs," Trabert said.

One ironworker said operations had been under way to raise the crane to finish off the new high-rise office building.

"The crane operator was swinging the crane around and someone shouted, 'Stop the swinging,'" one ironworker said.

Art Biada, a construction worker who had been on the job in the basement of the new building, said there was "a pretty wild noise." He added, "They were raising their crane and somebody made a mistake."

The back of the school bus was crushed. A cab also was smashed, but the driver, Gerald Smith, managed to scramble out through a window and his passengers were freed by workers.

The dead ironworkers included the crane operator. Firefighters said the other two ironworkers had been in the vicinity of the crane cab.

Ray Cortez, 51, Daly City, Calif., was standing next to his cement truck when he heard a loud noise above him. He said he dived under his truck. "You only have maybe three seconds," he said. "You heard the noise and knew you had to do something." His truck was smashed by falling debris.

A gasoline can on the street burst into flames when struck by debris. The fire was quickly extinguished. A pedestrian walkway was flattened.

The workers on the 10th floor of one of the struck buildings were evacuated immediately. Some suffered minor injuries.

Crews had been attempting to boost the crane to add another floor to a planned 20-story building—a job a union official described as usually dangerous. The accident occurred at California and Kearney Streets. The area is served by cable cars but none was involved in the disaster.

"As they jump it (raise a crane), the possibility of accidents increases," said Dennis Madigan, business manager of Ironworkers Local 377.

Bob O'Reilly of New Canaan, Conn., said he was in a cab when the driver shouted. He said they jumped out and took refuge under an archway.

"We just bailed out and got out of there," he said.

Officials at San Francisco General Hospital said 11 people were taken to the emergency room for treatment. They said three were admitted in serious condition. One was the Samtrans Bus driver, another was a construction worker. The third was a 12-year-old boy hurt while he awaited a bus.

A hospital official said the boy had "a lot of glass embedded in his face and scalp."

It was the second major incident in two days in the Bay Area, which is still recovering from the disastrous Oct. 17 earthquake. Two people died and six others were injured Monday night when a bus chartered by ABC Television was struck by a commuter train at a South San Francisco rail crossing.

Story 3:

This wire copy tells us far more than we care to know, but we're grateful that it provides plenty of names, dates, places, numbers and quotations, if not excitement. But that's the nature of most news; it's not the fault of the news agency. A lot of news is humdrum. Our job is to write it the best way we can. And do the best we know how. Make this story 20 seconds long, for the audience of a national newscast. Time to write: 20 minutes.

WASHINGTON (AP) — Amtrak will "starve to death" unless Congress identifies new funding to replace dwindling congressional allocations for the nation's passenger rail service, Amtrak's chairman told a Senate panel today.

During a Senate Commerce subcommittee hearing, Amtrak President Thomas Downs said funding cuts, combined with Congress' failure to identify a new funding source and allow for operational savings, are squeezing the rail service.

"Without the capital source and without legislative reform, we are dabbling with the edges of disaster for Amtrak," Downs said. "It will actually starve to death over the next five or six years."

Downs' comments came as lawmakers questioned Amtrak's plan to cancel four routes later this year.

"It can't be considered good policy to weaken the overall system in that way," said Sen. Kay Bailey Hutchison, R-Texas, chairwoman of the Surface Transportation and Merchant Marine Subcommittee. Downs agreed.

"I don't like losing any element of the system," he said. "I believe it weakens the national system."

But Amtrak faces a $243 million shortfall next year, Downs noted, even as Congress is contemplating a $50 million cut in federal subsidies. In a bid to save $200 million, the rail service has targeted four routes for elimination as of Nov. 10.

The lines are:

Texas Eagle, three-times-weekly service between Chicago, St. Louis, Little Rock, Dallas, Fort Worth and San Antonio, will be discontinued between St. Louis and San Antonio.

Pioneer, three-times-weekly service between Chicago, Denver, Portland, Ore., and Seattle, will be discontinued between Denver and Seattle.

Desert Wind, three-times-weekly between Chicago, Denver, Salt Lake City, Las Vegas and Los Angeles will be discontinued between Salt Lake City and Los Angeles.

Lake Shore Limited, daily between Chicago, Boston and New York, will be eliminated between Boston and Albany, N.Y.

Asked by Hutchison and Sen. Ron Wyden, D-Ore., if the eliminations could be delayed for six months, Downs replied: "I haven't got the resources to do it.... I cannot give what I haven't got."

Congress and the Clinton administration have directed Amtrak to achieve operating self-sufficiency by 2002. Even as Congress has cut Amtrak's federal operating support nearly 50 percent since fiscal 1995, lawmakers have yet to earmark a new funding source.

And, the rail service continues to await congressional approval of legislation that would allow it to greatly cut energy, labor and liability costs while gaining new freedom from red tape. The bill, which passed the House last year, remains mired in Senate squabbles.

Hutchison expressed support for one proposal: earmarking a half-cent from the 4.3-cent gasoline tax for Amtrak.

Story 4:

Please write 20 seconds. Take 15 minutes. Note: this story broke on a Friday but didn't move on the wires until Saturday. You are writing it for a Saturday night audience.

MINNEAPOLIS (AP) — Drinking five or more cups of coffee a day appears to increase a person's chances of developing lung cancer, according to a researcher who says his study is the first to target coffee alone.

"This is the first time that coffee has been implicated by itself" as a factor in lung cancer, Dr. Leonard Schuman, an epidemiologist at the University of Minnesota, said Friday.

He said the study also found that the effects of coffee drinking and smoking may magnify each other.

Smoking alone increases the risk of cancer tenfold, Schuman said. But men who smoked a pack or more a day and drank five or more cups of coffee had a rate of lung cancer 40 times higher than men who neither smoked nor drank coffee.

Other studies will be needed to determine if the finding represents a cause-and-effect relationship, or is just a fluke finding from one statistical study, Schuman said.

The study didn't ask people to distinguish between regular and decaffeinated coffee, so that's another question that further research might tackle, he said.

Harvard University researchers in 1981 found a statistical link between coffee drinking and pancreatic cancer, but later studies have virtually killed that theory.

Schuman and his colleagues have been studying the dietary habits of 17,818 men, all age 45 and older, and tracking their death rates over the past 18 years.

Even after smoking habits and ages were taken into consideration, those who drank five or more cups of coffee a day were seven times more likely to have died from lung cancer than the men who drank no coffee at all, Schuman said.

"On the basis of this one study, I don't think it's warranted to say 'ban coffee from your diet,'" Schuman said after the findings were reported at a Society for Epidemiologic Research meeting in Chapel Hill, N.C. However, moderation in many other things, might be prudent for many reasons," he added. "Smoking is still the most important factor in lung cancer," said Schuman.

He served on the U.S. Surgeon General's blue-ribbon committee of experts in 1964 that concluded that smoking is a major health risk.

Schuman's colleagues in the study are Dr. Robert Gibson of the University of Minnesota-Duluth and Dr. Erik Bjelke, who now lives in Norway.

Schuman said he didn't know what chemical in coffee might be responsible for any cancer risk, but it presumably would have to enter the bloodstream to reach the lungs.

Story 5:

By now, you probably see the best way to attack a story: go straight to the subject, go right to the verb and then to the object. Good old S-V-O: just the facts, no frills. So, on to this story. Make it 20 seconds, and try to write it in 25 minutes. Or less.

LOS ANGELES — More than 250 firefighters battled a stubborn, smoky fire that swept through the Central Los Angeles Library today, injuring 22 firefighters and destroying thousands of books in the downtown landmark building.

Neither Mayor Tom Bradley nor Fire Chief Donald Manning could say what caused the fire, which broke out shortly before 11 a.m. in the book stacks. It was declared under control six hours later, after 49 fire companies from across the city fought the blaze.

The 60-year-old library, which had 2.3 million volumes, was listed on the National Register of Historic Places and was declared a historic cultural monument by the Los Angeles Cultural Heritage board in 1967.

But the three-story building had also been designated as unsafe by the Los Angeles Fire Department and had a long history of fire violations. Mayor Bradley said some of the violations had been corrected, and library officials said fire doors were being installed when the fire broke out.

The interior of the library, which is situated amid a canyon of glass skyscrapers in downtown Los Angeles, was severely damaged. But its facade, although blackened and scorched, remained intact, in part because it was built of concrete, fire officials said.

"This is the most extremely difficult fire we have ever fought," Chief Manning said. "The men could not advance without the fire flaring up behind them."

The future of the library has been the topic of civic debate for the last 20 years. But, while various proposals were debated, the library began to fall into neglect, officials said.

About two years ago, a complicated plan involving the construction of three major buildings and the expansion of the library was worked out among private and public officials. The library staff was scheduled to move out next year for the expansion to begin.

Mayor Bradley, who arrived at the scene at 5 p.m., told reporters: "This magnificent building is something we have tried to save. We tried to get it up to safety standards."

Until the damage can be examined, the library's future is in doubt, the Mayor said, adding, "We will then decide whether to try to save it or to go forward with the remodeling."

Library officials said more than 300 employees and visitors were evacuated within minutes of the fire alarm sounding. Despite its landmark status, Chief Manning said, the building had no modern sprinkler system.

According to Robert Reagan, the library's public information director, steel fire doors were in the process of being installed between the book stacks and the public areas when the fire broke out. About half the work had been completed, he said.

Reagan said the library, the largest in the West, was "designated unsafe by the Fire Department as early as 1979." Violations were not corrected, he said, largely because of a lack of funds and uncertainty about its future.

The major fire violations, he said, were in the stacks that contained 85 percent of the library's books. The public has no direct access to the stacks.

The building, designed by the architect Bertram Grosvenor Goodhue and dedicated in 1926, was one of the few remaining buildings with open space in what is now the city's financial district.

From balconies and plazas of the glass skyscrapers that envelop the library, hundreds of office workers spent their lunch hour watching as smoke poured from the library's windows.

Firefighters were hampered by two factors: the desire to keep water at a minimum to decrease the water damage to the books and the fact that, for several hours, they were unable to bore a hole through the library's concrete roof to let the heat and smoke escape.

"It was like walking into a solid brick oven" said Capt. Anthony Didomenico of the Los Angeles Fire Department. Most of the injuries were caused by steam burns.

By day's end, neither fire officials nor library officials could estimate the amount of damage. The rare book collection, which is kept in a fireproof vault in the building's basement, was believed to be unharmed. But the general collection of books, many of which Reagan described as "irreplaceable," were probably ruined.

"We have a great collection of books here," he said. "How can I put a price on what is a priceless collection?"

Story 6:

On to the next exercise. Or scrimmage. This is a complex story to compress, and it offers a writer many chances to fumble—and to score. Write a 25-second story. This time, try to write it in less than 25 minutes. And try not to go into overtime.

WASHINGTON — Using free Washington Redskins tickets as bait, authorities arrested 100 fugitives who showed up Sunday at a pre-game brunch where police and federal marshals posed as waiters and served warrants.

U.S. marshals called it the largest mass arrest of fugitives in recent memory.

"It was like an assembly line," said Herbert M. Rutherford III, U.S. marshal for the District of Columbia. "It was party time, and they fell for it, hook, line and sinker."

"This ain't fair, this just ain't fair," said one prisoner who was led in handcuffs from one of the two large buses that carried the prisoners to a local jail.

"They said they was takin' us to a football game, and that's wrong," said another man. "That's false advertising."

"I came to see Boomer, I came to see Boomer," said a third, referring to Cincinnati Bengals quarterback Boomer Esiason.

U.S. marshals, working with the Metropolitan Police Department, sent out invitations to 3,000 wanted persons. The invitations said that as a promotion for a new sports television station, Flagship International Sports Television, they were winners of two free

tickets to the National Football League game Sunday
between the Redskins and the Bengals.

The invitation said 10 of the "lucky winners" would
receive season tickets to the Redskins' 1986 season and
that a grand prize drawing would be held for an all-
expenses paid trip to the upcoming Super Bowl XX in New
Orleans.

The initials for the TV enterprise, F.I.S.T., also
stand for the Fugitive Investigative Strike Team, a
special U.S. marshals force.

About 100 fugitives responded to the invitation and
appeared at the D.C. Convention Center for the special
brunch. The building was decorated with signs saying,
"Let's party" and "Let's all be there."

Some of the fugitives showed up wearing the bright
burgundy-and-gold wool Redskins hats as well as
Redskins buttons, while others were attired in suits
and ties for the pre-game feast.

One marshal was dressed in a large yellow chicken
suit with oversized red boots while another turned up
as an Indian chief complete with large headdress.

Other marshals wearing tuxedos handed small name
stickers to each of the fugitives.

Buses that were to take them to the game, however,
took them to the police department's central cellblock
several blocks away instead.

"When we verified their identity, we escorted them
in small groups to a party room, where officers moved in

from concealed positions and placed them under arrest,"
said Stanley Morris, head of the U.S. Marshals Service.

The sting netted 100 fugitives by 11 a.m., marshals
said.

Arrested were two people wanted for murder, five for
robbery, 15 for assault, six for burglary, 19 for bond
or bail violations, 18 for narcotics violations,
officials said. Others were arrested on charges of rape,
arson and forgery. Two of those arrested were on the
D.C. police department's ten most wanted list.

A similar scam in Hartford, Conn., in November 1984
invited people to attend a luncheon with pop singer Boy
George. Fifteen were picked up by limousine and
arrested. Marshals said they used job offers as the
bait to arrest about 90 people in Brooklyn last year.

"Redskin tickets are valuable. And when you're
trying to get a person, you play on their greed," said
Toby Roche, chief deputy U.S. marshal for Washington,
who coordinated the operation.

The cost of the project was estimated to be
$22,100, or about $225 per arrest.

One man who got into the Convention Center before
apparently being spooked by the circumstances was
arrested on the street, still wearing his "Hello, my
name is...." sticker.

Story 7:

Yes, this story is dated. But for our purposes, the story is as good now as the day the baby was born. It still puts us to the test, gives a workout to our mental muscles, and teaches us a few lessons about writing news. Now, try your hand at this one, 20 seconds in 15 minutes for a Sunday night newscast.

LONDON (AP) — Smiling to a cheering crowd, Princess Diana took home from the hospital Sunday her one-day-old son, Henry Charles Albert David.

The baby, third in line to the British throne, will be known to his family simply as Harry.

Diana, 23, wore a red coat and cradled the infant swathed in a white shawl as she left the hospital 22 hours after a routine birth. Her husband, Prince Charles, 35, accompanied Diana and their new son home to their London residence, Kensington Palace.

The princess blushed as the crowd of about 1,000 people, some of whom had waited through the night outside London's St Mary's Hospital, waved Union Jacks and called out, "Hurrah, Harry!"

The royal couple's first child, two-year-old Prince William, visited his mother and baby brother for 15 minutes earlier.

William, looking confused by the phalanx of photographers, arrived with Charles, but left holding the hand of his nanny, Barbara Barnes. He gave three small waves to a delighted crowd.

The baby, taken home in a three-car motorcade at the start of a life of wealth, privilege and constant

publicity, bears the name of England's famed Henry
VIII, who broke with Rome in 1534 because the Vatican
would not give him a divorce.

"They chose the name Henry simply because they both
like it and also because there is no other member of
the royal family at present with that name," said a
Buckingham Palace spokesman. "The other names all have
family connections."

Prayers of thanksgiving were offered at Sunday
church services around the country in this strongly
monarchist nation for the birth of Prince Henry, who
ranks behind Charles and William in the line of
succession. He joins them as a Prince of Wales.

Bells pealed for three hours Sunday across the
Gloucestershire village of Tetbury, where Charles and
Diana have their country residence, Highgrove House.

The palace said the royal family will call the new
prince Harry. The affectionate diminutive is in
contrast to palace instructions that William must never
be referred to as Bill, or Willy.

The new baby's second name, Charles, is both the
name of his father and of Diana's only brother,
Viscount Althorp, 21. Albert was the first name of the
baby's great-grandfather, who reigned as George VI, and
of Queen Victoria's consort.

David, a palace announcement said, was for
Elizabeth the Queen Mother's favorite brother, the late
Sir David Bowes-Lyons. David was also one of the names
of Charles' great-uncle, Edward VIII, who abdicated in

1936 to marry a twice-divorced American, Wallis Simpson.

"The baby is fine! My wife is even better!" Charles shouted to the crowd outside the hospital after a three-hour morning visit Saturday.

The speed of the announcement of the names of the 6-pound, 14-ounce baby aroused speculation the princess knew from medical tests that it would be another boy.

William's names, William Arthur Phillip Louis, were not announced until a week after his birth in the same private ward at St. Mary's on June 21, 1982.

Charles was with Diana, the daughter of Earl Spencer and a former kindergarten teacher whom he married July 29, 1981, throughout her nine-hour labor and the birth Saturday.

Queen Elizabeth II was due back in London next Friday from her Scottish residence, Balmoral, said a palace spokesman, who spoke on condition he not be identified.

The queen smiled and waved to villagers Sunday when she attended church in the nearby Scottish hamlet of Crathie. Prayers were offered for the baby, her fourth grandchild. Her only daughter, Princess Anne, 33, has two children, Peter and Zara Phillips.

The new prince pushes Charles' brothers, Andrew, 24, and Edward, 20, into fourth and fifth in the line of succession. Anne is now sixth.

Story 8:

Write this story for early evening, Tuesday, before the Pope makes his first stop. Length: 20 seconds. Time: 15 minutes.

VATICAN CITY (UPI) — Pope John Paul II left Rome Tuesday for his 32nd foreign tour, traveling to Bangladesh, Singapore, Fiji, New Zealand, Australia and the Seychelles on his longest and one of his most grueling trips.

The Pontiff, who left Rome's Leonardo da Vinci Airport 20 minutes behind schedule, will spend the night on his jet and land early Wednesday in the Bangladesh capital of Dhaka, where he will make 12 hours of public appearances.

John Paul will be traveling virtually non-stop to cover the 30,000-mile itinerary in 14 days, and is to spend two of the first three nights sleeping aboard the papal plane to save time.

Among the highlights of the trip are scheduled meetings with native Fiji islanders, New Zealand Maoris and Australian aborigines, whose numbers and culture were nearly eliminated after European settlers arrived in the late 18th century.

Each of the three groups is scheduled to give John Paul a traditional welcome. In Fiji he is to receive a whale tooth, the local version of the key to a city, and sip a watered-down version of kava, the powerful local brew.

In New Zealand, he will touch noses with a group of Maori tribesman as a sign of trust, and in Australia, aborigines will lead him along a traditional "meeting path" as various tribes perform native dances and songs.

The trip — longest both in terms of distance and days spent outside the Vatican — is the third to Asia and the Pacific since he became pope in 1978. Half the trip will be spent in Australia, with three days in New Zealand and the remaining four days on brief stops in Bangladesh, Singapore, Fiji and the Seychelles.

The Dhaka stop, during which John Paul is to ordain local priests and celebrate Mass for the country's tiny Catholic minority, could take on an unexpected inter-religious significance, a senior Vatican official said shortly before the trip.

A Moslem leader in Bangladesh recently contacted the Vatican and asked to be present at the religious services as a goodwill gesture in response to the Pope's address to Moslem youth in Casablanca in August 1985, and last month's inter- religious prayer meeting for peace in Assisi, Italy.

"This is the first time a Moslem leader has responded in such a way," the source said.

In Australia and New Zealand, church attendance has fallen off drastically in recent years and the supply of priests is fast dwindling.

Recent Australian polls show that less than 30 percent of the nation's 4 million Catholics attend Sunday Mass, while church members, as in other highly developed nations, widely ignore Rome's ban on artificial contraception.

Story 9:

This is another golden oldie, but for us it's still as good as gold. The producer of your Sunday night network newscast tells you she wants it 20 seconds long. Time for you to write: 15 minutes.

LONDON (AP) — Smuggled letters from Soviet dissident Andrei Sakharov reveal that he has been mentally and physically tortured by Soviet secret police while in internal exile in the closed city of Gorky, the weekly Observer reported Sunday.

The newspaper said the documents "unmask the careful plan of KGB disinformation," including postcards and telegrams carrying his wife's name, that have for nearly two years suggested Sakharov was living without problems.

Sakharov's stepdaughter, Tatyana Yankelevich, and her husband, Yefrem, received the smuggled letters and photographs in two plain envelopes mailed from an unidentified Western country to the couple in Newton, Mass., the Observer said.

It quoted Yankelevich as saying, "How they got out of the Soviet Union I cannot say, but I know the source, and the source is reliable. They (the documents) have been carefully examined by the whole family and we are convinced of their authenticity."

Yankelevich, contacted in Newton by The Associated Press, confirmed that he had provided the Observer with the documents. "There were some financial arrangements, but I won't be able to discuss it," he said.

Sakharov, a physicist who led fellow scientists to produce the Soviet hydrogen bomb, has been in internal exile in Gorky, 260 miles east of Moscow, since January 1980.

He became a human rights activist in the 1960s and was ordered to Gorky after he publicly criticized the Soviets' military intervention in Afghanistan in December 1979.

The Observer said the letters, which it will publish in extract starting next week, detail the KGB's ill treatment of Sakharov. They confirm reports that Sakharov was force-fed during two hunger strikes in 1984 and 1985 and was subjected to mental torture and physical violence while being treated at a Gorky Hospital, it said.

The KGB is the Soviet security police and intelligence agency. Sakharov spent several months on a hunger strike in an effort to get an exit visa for his wife, Yelena Bonner.

The paper said the main document is a 20-page letter written by Sakharov in October 1984 to Dr. Anatoli Alexandrov, president of the Soviet Academy of Sciences. In it, Sakharov appeals for his wife to be allowed to go to the West for medical treatment. Mrs. Bonner was granted an exit visa late last year, and she is now in Massachusetts, where she underwent a heart bypass operation.

Sakharov also describes how he was seized by KGB agents on May 7, 1984, and taken to Gorky's Semashko hospital, the paper said.

Sakharov wrote that hospital authorities "kept me by force and tormented me for four months. My attempts to flee the hospital were always blocked by KGB men, who were on duty round the clock to bar all means of escape," according to the Observer.

It said the letters "contain one of the most vivid testimonies of human suffering ever to have emerged in the Soviet Union."

EXERCISES IN
WRITING BROADCAST NEWS CD-ROM

Accompanying this book is a CD-ROM designed for use with both PC and Macintosh computers. In any case, you will need a color screen. If the text on your screen appears too small, go to the Control Panel and adjust your Display resolution to 640x480. The installation instructions and specific requirements are listed below.

Windows 95 / Windows NT Workstation 4.0

You will need 8MB free disk space.

Run *setup.exe* from the Exercises in Writing Broadcast News CD-ROM to install the program on your hard drive.

Once the program is installed, an icon called WBNews should appear in the Programs submenu of the Start menu. Select this icon to start the program.

You can get help any time while running the program by pressing <F1>.

Macintosh

The Writing Broadcast News program can be run directly from the CD-ROM by double-clicking on the Writing Broadcast News icon.

Help is available in html form in the file *wbnews-help.html,* which can be viewed using a web browser. Help is also available in plain text form in the *wbnews* help file.

INDEX

149

Mervin Block has worked as a staff writer on the "CBS Evening News" and "ABC Evening News," and has freelanced at NBC News.

He has written for Ed Bradley, Tom Brokaw, Walter Cronkite, Charles Kuralt, Charles Osgood, Dan Rather, Frank Reynolds, Diane Sawyer and Mike Wallace.

Block has written and broadcast editorials, WNBC-TV, New York City; served as executive news producer, WBBM-TV, Chicago; and won first prize three times for TV spot-news scripts in the annual competition of the Writers Guild. He has also written a column for the RTNDA *Communicator.*

Earlier, he was a newspaper reporter and editor in Chicago.

He holds the M.S.J. from the Medill School of Journalism and a certificate from Columbia University's Graduate School of Journalism, where he has taught broadcast newswriting. And he has been teaching workshops at TV and radio stations.

Joe Durso, Jr., taught broadcast newswriting at the University of Montana, served as chairman of the Department of Radio-Television and was about to begin his third year as acting dean of the School of Journalism. But shortly before publication of this book, he died of a heart attack.

Dean Durso started his career as a reporter for "Newsroom" on WETA-TV, PBS, Washington, D.C. He wrote and broadcast editorials at WCBS-AM, New York City, the all-news CBS Radio flagship, and later was news director there; served as director of the CBS Radio Station News Service, Washington, D.C.; and worked as news director, WBBM-AM, Chicago, an all-news CBS O&O.

He was co-author of *Growing Up Western,* describing the life of a boy in Montana during the Depression.

Dean Durso held the M.S.J. from Columbia University's Graduate School of Journalism.